D1242004

SCREEN ADAPTATIONS
SHAKESPEARE'S
THE TEMPEST
THE RELATIONSHIP BETWEEN TEXT AND FILM

LISA HOPKINS

methuen | drama

1 3 5 7 9 10 8 6 4 2

First published 2008

Methuen Drama
A & C Black Publishers Limited
38 Soho Square
London W1D 3HB
www.acblack.com
ISBN 978-0-7136-7910-6

A CIP catalogue record for this book is available
from the British Library

This book is produced using paper made from wood grown in
managed, sustainable forests. It is natural, renewable and
recyclable. The logging and manufacturing processes conform
to the environmental regulations of the country of origin.

Printed and bound in Great Britain by
CPI Cox & Wyman, Reading, Berkshire

contents

....

Dedication

In fond memory of Archie Markham.

Acknowledgements

Thanks to Deborah Cartmell, Andrew Glewis, Kirsten Law, Paul Stewart, and Bob White – and most of all, as always, to Chris and Sam Hopkins.

A note on texts

All quotations from *The Tempest* are taken from William Shakespeare, *The Tempest*, edited by Virginia Mason Vaughan and Alden T. Vaughan (London: Thomas Nelson and Sons, 1999).

credits/filmography

••

Credits for key films

Forbidden Planet (1956)

Director   Fred M. Wilcox
Writers   Irving Block and Allen Adler

Main cast
Walter Pidgeon   Dr Edward Morbius
Anne Francis   Altaira Morbius
Leslie Nielsen   Commander John J. Adams
Warren Stevens   Lt 'Doc' Ostrow
Jack Kelly   Lt Jerry Farman
Richard Anderson   Chief Engineer Quinn
Earl Holliman   James Dirocco, the cook
Robby the Robot   Robby, The Robot
George Wallace   Bosun
Robert Dix   Grey (as Bob Dix)
Jimmy Thompson   Youngerford
James Drury   Joe Strong
Harry Harvey Jr   Randall
Roger McGee   Lindstrom
Peter Miller   Moran

The Tempest (1979)

Director	Derek Jarman
Writers	Derek Jarman and William Shakespeare

Main Cast

Peter Bull	Alonso, the King of Naples
David Meyer	Ferdinand, his son
Neil Cunningham	Sebastian, his brother
Heathcote Williams	Prospero, the Right Duke of Milan
Toyah Willcox	Miranda, his daughter
Richard Warwick	Antonio, his brother
Karl Johnson	Ariel, an airy spirit
Jack Birkett	Caliban, a savage and deformed slave
Christopher Biggins	Stephano, a drunken mariner
Peter Turner	Trinculo, his friend
Ken Campbell	Gonzalo, an honest councillor
Elisabeth Welch	A Goddess
Claire Davenport	Sycorax
Kate Temple	Young Miranda
Helen Wellington-Lloyd	A Spirit

Prospero's Books (1991)

Director	Peter Greenaway
Writers	William Shakespeare and Peter Greenaway

Main cast

John Gielgud	Prospero
Michael Clark	Caliban
Michel Blanc	Alonso
Erland Josephson	Gonzalo
Isabelle Pasco	Miranda
Tom Bell	Antonio
Kenneth Cranham	Sebastian
Mark Rylance	Ferdinand
Gerard Thoolen	Adrian
Pierre Bokma	Francisco
Jim van der Woude	Trinculo
Michiel Romeyn	Stephano
Orpheo	Ariel
Paul Russell	Ariel
James Thiérrée	Ariel

Other films referred to

2001: A Space Odyssey (1968) Directed by Stanley Kubrick for Metro-Goldwyn-Mayer.

A Midsummer Night's Dream (1935) Directed by Max Reinhardt for Warner Bros.

A Midsummer Night's Dream (1984) Directed by Celestino Coronado for Cabochon.

Caravaggio (1986) Directed by Derek Jarman for the British Film Institute.

Edward II (1991) Directed by Derek Jarman for the British Broadcasting Corporation.

Fight Club (1999) Directed by David Fincher for Art Linson Productions.

Gone With the Wind (1939) Directed by Victor Fleming for Selznick International Pictures.

Gremlins (1984) Directed by Joe Dante for Amblin Entertainment.

Hotel (2001) Directed by Mike Figgis for Cattleya.

Iguana (1988) Directed by Monte Hellman for Arco Films.

Invasion of the Body Snatchers (1956) Directed by Don Siegel for Walter Wanger Productions.

Island of Lost Souls (1932) Directed by Eric C. Kenton for Paramount Pictures.

Jubilee (1977) Directed by Derek Jarman for Megalovision.

Lassie Come Home (1943) Directed by Fred M. Wilcox for Loew's.

Never on Sunday (1960) Directed by Jules Dassin for Lopert Pictures Corporation.

Nosferatu (1922) Directed by F. W. Murnau for Jofa-Atelier Berlin-Johannisthal.

Pocahontas (1995) Directed by Mike Gabriel and Eric Goldberg for Walt Disney Feature Animation.

Requiem for Methuselah (1969) Directed by Murray Golden as episode 76 of *Star Trek* series one.

Resan till Melonia (1989) Directed by Per Åhlin for PennFilm Studio.

Robocop (1987) Directed by Paul Verhoeven for Orion Pictures Corporation.

Tempest (1982) Directed by Paul Mazursky for Columbia Pictures Corporation.

The Belly of an Architect (1987) Directed by Peter Greenaway for British Screen Hemdale.

The Draughtsman's Contract (1982) Directed by Peter Greenaway for the British Film Institute.

The Invisible Boy (1957) Directed by Herman Hoffman for Metro-Goldwyn-Mayer.

The Lord of the Rings: The Two Towers (2002) Directed by Peter Jackson for New Line Cinema.

The Lord of the Rings: The Return of the King (2003) Directed by Peter Jackson for New Line Cinema.

The Running Man (1987) Directed by Paul Michael Glaser for Braveworld Productions.

The Tempest (1908) Directed by Percy Stow for the Clarendon Film Company.

The Tempest (1939) Directed by Dallas Bower for the British Broadcasting Corporation.

The Tempest (1980) Directed by John Gorrie for the British Broadcasting Corporation.

The Tempest (1992) Directed by Stanislav Sokolov for Christmas Films.

The Tempest (1998) Directed by Jack Bender for Bonnie Raskin Productions.

The Wizard of Oz (1939) Directed by Victor Fleming for Metro-Goldwyn-Mayer.

William Shakespeare's Romeo + Juliet (1996) Directed by Baz Lurhmann for Bazmark Films.

Yellow Sky (1949) Directed by William A. Wellman for Twentieth-Century Fox.

Zorba the Greek (1964) Directed by Mihalis Kakogiannis for Rochley.

Television series

Babylon 5
Lost in Space
Star Trek

PART 1:
Literary contexts

the play in its time

··

The first recorded performance of *The Tempest* took place on 1 November 1611, in the presence of King James I, at court. As John G. Demaray points out, 'The second and the only other documented performance of the play in Shakespeare's lifetime was again before King James at Whitehall in 1613, in celebration of the marriage of the King's daughter, Princess Elizabeth, to Frederick Elector ... Palatine, a Protestant prince noted for his occultist views and associations'.[1] One can easily see why *The Tempest* was chosen for this occasion. Not only did the Elector, as Demaray notes, have an interest in magic himself – his later capital of Prague was famous as the principal centre for magic in Europe – but the play's central focus on the marriage of a royal and beautiful young couple makes it obviously appropriate for the event.

However, although *The Tempest* fitted this event well, the immediate prompt for Shakespeare to write it – probably in late 1610 or early 1611 – was not the marriage of the princess but the wreck of the English ship the *Sea Venture* on the coast of Bermuda in 1609, while it was on its way to the fledgling Jamestown colony

[1] John G. Demaray, *Shakespeare and the Spectacles of Strangeness* (Pittsburgh: Duquesne University Press, 1998), p. 4.

in Virginia. A number of verbal details in the play can be traced back to William Strachey's pamphlet *A True Reportory of the Wreck and Redemption of Sir Thomas Gates, Knight*, which gave an account of the wreck of the *Sea Venture* and the subsequent experiences of those on board during their time in Bermuda. This is clearly the source for the description of Ariel flaming on the masthead at I.ii.196-201:

> I boarded the King's ship; now on the beak,
> Now in the waist, the deck, in every cabin
> I flamed amazement. Sometime I'd divide
> And burn in many places; on the topmast,
> The yards and bowsprit would I flame distinctly,
> Then meet and join.

Strachey had reported that

> ... on the Thursday night, Sir George Summers being upon the watch, had an apparition of a little round light, like a faint star, trembling, and streaming along with a sparkling blaze, half the height upon the mainmast, and shooting sometimes from shroud to shroud, tempting to settle as it were upon any of the four shrouds.

Strachey also seems to lie behind Caliban's reference to 'Water with berries in't' (I.ii.335), since he speaks of 'the berries whereof our men, seething, straining, and letting stand some three or four days, made a kind of pleasant drink'.[2]

---

[2] William Strachey, 'A True Reportory...', in *A Voyage to Virginia in 1609: Two Narratives: Strachey's "True Reportory", Jourdain's Discovery of the Bermudas* (Charlottesville: University Press of Virginia, 1964), p. 24.

Shakespeare's choice of source was an interesting one. Many modern analyses have related *The Tempest* to the history of colonialism, but less often mentioned is the fact that Strachey's *True Reportory* was not in any sense a 'standard' take on the subject. In fact, it had been such bad propaganda for the Virginia Company that it had effectively been suppressed:

> ... the Virginia Company was doing its best to discount unfavourable reports coming back from the New World and was carrying on a campaign of propaganda to convince the public that the Virginian enterprise was still potentially profitable. Strachey's narrative was therefore too realistic in its picture of the unhappy conditions in the colony to make it publishable and it had to wait fifteen years until Purchas put it into print.[3]

Although Strachey does pay lip-service to the idea of future travel to Virginia, exhorting would-be colonists to 'let no rumor of the poverty of the country ... waive any man's fair purposes hitherward',[4] his editor points out that 'His narration of the shortcomings of some of the group and of the mutinies that nearly ruined their prospects of escaping from the Bermudas were not matters that the Virginia Company of London would want to publish abroad'.[5]

In particular, Strachey plays the rhetorical game of apparently dismissing something while nevertheless bringing it forcefully to his readers' attention, when he refers to a particularly unpleasant event that had occurred in the new colony – 'the tragical history

[3] William Strachey, *The Historie of Travell into Virginia Britania* (1612), edited by Louis B. Wright and Virginia Freund (London: The Hakluyt Society, 1953), introduction, p. xxii.
[4] Strachey, *Reportory*, p. 69.
[5] Strachey, *Reportory*, p. xiv.

of the man eating of his dead wife in Virginia'.[6] Although he says that this occurred because the husband disliked the wife, not because he was driven to desperation by a shortage of food in the colony, the damage is obviously done. Moreover, though Strachey tends to speak favourably of the numerous small islands that collectively make up Bermuda, he also observes that 'they be so terrible to all that ever touched on them, and such tempests, thunders, and other fearful objects are seen and heard about them, that they be called commonly the Devil's Islands'.[7] Finally, Strachey draws attention to the work of a notable sceptic of the benefits and justification of colonisation when he refers to 'those small worms which Acosta writeth of'.[8] This refers to José de Acosta, whose 1590 *Historia natural y moral de las Indias* questioned Spain's right to enslave and mistreat the indigenous inhabitants of the Americas.

There are, then, general issues of colonisation and exploration at stake in Strachey's narrative as well as an account of a particular event, and *The Tempest*'s borrowings from Strachey mean that the play cries out to be read in the context of the growing push towards mapping and exploiting the New World. Indeed while, as Susan Bennett observes, 'the textual body of Shakespeare's plays has been a prevalent and enduring component of Western colonial practice' in general, 'No Western text has played a more visible role in the representation and reconstruction of the colonial body than Shakespeare's *The Tempest*'.[9]

[6] Strachey, *Repertory*, p. 97.

[7] Strachey, *Repertory*, p. 16.

[8] Strachey, *Repertory*, p. 25.

[9] Susan Bennett, *Performing Nostalgia: Shifting Shakespeare and the Contemporary Past* (London: Routledge, 1996), pp. 123 and 119.

Colonisation was not simply a question of conquering new lands, and many of the other issues on which it touched are also relevant to *The Tempest*. One discourse significantly inflected by the experiences of colonisation was that of sexuality and gender; indeed Elaine Showalter remarks that '(d)iscovered by an anatomist appropriately named Columbus in the sixteenth century, the Renaissance clitoris was the brave new world'.[10] It has often been remarked that in texts discussing the colonial enterprise, the colonised land and the female body are frequently perceived as analogous,[11] a parallelism which is neatly emblematised in the double use of the metaphor of 'dis/covery' both for voyages of exploration and for the exposure of the female body. In particular, in almost all Elizabethan and Jacobean writing on Ireland, the closest of the colonies, images of monstrous femininity figured very prominently, and it is worth noting at this point that even though it is never mentioned in *The Tempest*, Ireland has been suggested by some recent critics as an important context for the play. Ireland itself was often represented as a woman, as in this description by Luke Gernon:

[10] Elaine Showalter, *Sexual Anarchy: Gender and Culture at the Fin de Siècle* [1990] (London: Bloomsbury, 1991), p.130.

[11] Sir Walter Ralegh, for instance, referred to Guiana as 'a cuntry that hath yet her maidenhead'. The analogy in the case of *The Tempest* has been extensively discussed in, amongst other places, Francis Barker and Peter Hulme, 'Nymphs and reapers heavily vanish: the discursive con-texts of *The Tempest*', in *Alternative Shakespeares*, edited by John Drakakis (London: Methuen, 1985), pp. 191–205; by Paul Brown, '"This thing of darkness I acknowledge mine": *The Tempest* and the discourse of colonialism', in *Political Shakespeare*, edited by Jonathan Dollimore and Alan Sinfield (Manchester: Manchester University Press, 1985), pp. 48–71; and in Thomas Healy, *New Latitudes: Theory and English Renaissance Literature* (London: Edward Arnold, 1992), pp. 95 and 145.

> This Nymph of Ireland is at all poynts like a yong wenche that
> hath the greene sicknes for want of occupying. She is very fayre
> of visage, and hath a smooth skinn of tender grasse ... Her
> breasts are round hillockes of milk-yeelding grasse, and that so
> fertile, that they conten(d) with the vallyes. And betwixt her leggs
> (for Ireland is full of havens), she hath an open harbor, but not
> much frequented ... It is nowe since she was drawne out of the
> wombe of rebellion about sixteen yeares, by'rlady nineteen,
> and yet she wants a husband, she is not embraced, she is not
> hedged and ditched, there is noo quicksett putt into her.[12]

For Gernon, then, Ireland is a helpless maiden who can never be
satisfied until the English enter and possess her.

Gernon's image of Ireland as a nubile virgin desperate for sex
draws on a common Renaissance trope, which compares land to
be conquered to women to be married; the English were fond of
labelling Spanish colonial activity as rape while simultaneously
glorifying their own as 'husbandry', so that one Ulster poet praising
James VI and I wrote that 'Ireland (is) due to thee, thou are her
spouse by all the signs'.[13] As Lynda Boose comments,

> although the equation between land and the female body
> which makes rape and imperialism homologous is a metaphor of
> masculine ownership that is neither peculiarly English nor new to
> England's enclosure period, the collocation of the two discursive

[12] Andrew Hadfield and Willy Maley, 'Introduction: Irish representations and English
alternatives' in *Representing Ireland: Literature and the Origins of Conflict, 1534–
1660*, edited by Brendan Bradshaw, Andrew Hadfield, and Willy Maley
(Cambridge: Cambridge University Press, 1993), pp. 1–23, p. 4.
[13] Tristan Marshall, *Theatre and empire: Great Britain on the London stages under
James VI and I* (Manchester: Manchester University Press, 2000), p. 16.

fields clearly acquired new energy at precisely this historical moment of heightened land anxieties.[14]

The link between women and land is particularly pertinent in *The Tempest*. Susan Bennett argues that

Only when power is guaranteed is the colonizer prepared to evacuate the hitherto virgin territory (the island, his daughter's body). Miranda, then, is as much a colonial territory as the island she has been brought up on, and her reproductive body ensures for her father the re-production of his own power back in Milan.[15]

Although postcolonial readings of *The Tempest* have generally paid attention principally to Caliban, Miranda too is an important character to consider in this context.

For all her status as European princess, Miranda might in some respects also remind us of the native women on whom European travellers frequently commented. In particular, *The Tempest* has often been discussed in the the light of the story of Pocahontas, the young Native American girl who is famously supposed to have intervened to save the life of Captain John Smith after he was threatened with execution by her father Chief Powhatan, and who

[14] Lynda E. Boose, 'The Taming of the Shrew, Good Husbandry, and Enclosure', in *Shakespeare Reread: The Texts in New Contexts*, edited by Russ McDonald (Ithaca: Cornell University Press, 1994), pp. 193–225, p. 203. On the woman-land metaphor see also Virginia Mason Vaughan, 'Preface: The Mental Maps of English Renaissance Drama', in *Playing the Globe: Genre and Geography in English Renaissance Drama*, edited by John Gillies and Virginia Mason Vaughan (London: Associated University Presses, 1998), pp. 7–16, p. 12, and Louis Montrose, 'The Work of Gender in the Discourse of Discovery', *Representations* 33 (winter, 1991), pp. 1–41.
[15] Bennett, *Performing Nostalgia*, p. 127.

later went on to marry another Englishman, John Rolfe, and to visit England a few years after Shakespeare wrote *The Tempest*. Pocahontas is mentioned several times by William Strachey, author of the account of the wreck of *The Sea Venture*, and in the light of the similarities between her story and that of Miranda, her father, and her suitor, it is not surprising that Peter Hulme, for instance, remarks that 'The early history of the English colony of Virginia contains one story – perhaps its most famous – that has tantalizing parallels with *The Tempest*'.[16]

Both Miranda and Pocahontas show how, through her gender and her race, the woman is doubly the object of the appropriating colonial gaze – especially since her behaviour is often perceived as rendering her more remote from the norms of European femininity than the male native is from the male European.[17] While the colonised male can often be regarded as effectively the mirror image of his new master,[18] the female frequently appears to escape

[16] Peter Hulme, *Colonial Encounters: Europe and the Native Caribbean 1492–1797* (London: Methuen, 1986), p. 137.

[17] The link between femininity and monstrousness is discussed in Karen Newman, '"And wash the Ethiop white": femininity and the monstrous in *Othello*', in *Shakespeare Reproduced*, edited by Jean E. Howard and Marion F. O'Connor (London: Methuen, 1987), pp. 143–62.

[18] This is argued by Tzvetan Todorov in *The Conquest of America: The Question of the Other*, translated by R. Howard (New York: Doubleday, 1984), p. 42. Stephen Greenblatt similarly discusses 'the testing upon bodies and minds of non-Europeans or, more generally, the non-civilised, of a hypothesis about the origin and nature of European culture and belief' ('Invisible bullets: Renaissance authority and its subversion: *Henry IV* and *Henry V*', in *Political Shakespeare*, pp. 18–47, p. 22), and Malcolm Evans refers to 'the ideological mirror of the Americas which could reflect contradictory images – of the civilizations of the European face and also of its barbarism' (*Signifying Nothing: Truth's True Contents in Shakespeare's Texts*, 2nd edition [Hemel Hempstead: Harvester, 1989], p. 48).

all available forms of classification and response, as witnessed in the following comments by the early Italian observer Amerigo Vespucci, after whom America was named, on native women:

> They are women of pleasing person, very well proportioned, so that one does not see on their bodies any ill-formed feature or limb. And although they go about utterly naked, they are fleshy women, and that part of their privies which he has not seen them would think to see is invisible ... They showed themselves very desirous of copulating with us Christians.[19]

Here the female body appears actually to be biologically dissimilar from familiar norms, and the male gaze – in Vespucci's case, obviously quite a prolonged and intense one – finds itself ultimately resisted by its own inability to assimilate the visual information it receives to the pre-existing mental sets which determine how it sees.

At first glance, Shakespeare's Miranda appears to pose no such problem to the enquiring male eye. Her very name – to which her father's command so pointedly draws our attention – offers her up as an object to be effortlessly decoded: she is 'miranda', a Latin gerundive roughly translatable as 'she who must be admired'. To any educated male European that she might meet, her name would immediately label her in grammatical and semantic terms as passive, female, the object of the gaze. Her clearly demarcated status within both language and culture can, it seems, leave her nothing in common with the strange, non-European females

---

[19] Letter to Piero Soderini, quoted in *Culture and Belief in Europe 1450–1600: An Anthology of Sources*, edited by David Englander, Diana Norman, Rosemary O'Day and W. R. Owens (Oxford: Oxford University Press, 1990), p. 318.

whose inappropriate anatomy so determinedly resists the possessing male eye.

And yet Miranda, for all her position as princess of Milan and Prospero's daughter, can nevertheless be read as occupying a position which, to some extent at least, overlaps with that of the colonised female native. Like female natives, she has only the most fragmentary and second-hand experience of European culture; she has never lived in civilised society, and indeed can remember almost nothing outside the environs of the island on which they live; she has almost no experience of white men or women; her upbringing and environment are clearly analogous to those of Caliban, who can stand, albeit rather problematically, as an emblem of the colonised indigenous population; and perhaps most obviously of all, she has been firmly inserted into language as the object of the male gaze.

Miranda's situation is, in fact, extremely ambiguous. On one level she is that very rare phenomenon, a female coloniser – a fact which may strike us in the curious parallel between her own name and the name which King Ferdinand of Aragon is said to have proposed for that arch-coloniser, Christopher Columbus: 'the king of Spain said that Columbus should be called not *Almirante*, the admiral, but *Admirans*, the one who wonders'.[20] (The extent to which Miranda is implicated in the colonial enterprise – or more properly, the extent to which it has at various periods been acceptable to see her as such – is interestingly illustrated by the long-running editorial controversy over whether she or Prospero should be given the lines in which the speaker claims to have taught

[20] Stephen Greenblatt, *Marvelous Possessions* (Oxford: The Clarendon Press, 1991), p. 83. He also comments interestingly on the extent to which wonder and looking are central to the European response to the New World (pp. 14 and 77).

Caliban language. The First Folio allots the lines to Miranda, but some editors have felt this to be inappropriate and have transferred them to Prospero instead.)[21] As coloniser, Miranda functions as representative of her own culture, and yet her position within that culture is itself fraught with insecurity. Not only has she had no contact with any member of it other than her father Prospero, whose suitability to initiate her into it may perhaps be called into question, but she is, moreover, an oddity within the patriarchal society from which she originates, in that her status as only child of a duke is set to position her as that anomaly of Renaissance culture, a female ruler. The same tension is set up in those remarkable visual images of Elizabeth I, the Ditchley and Armada portraits, which show the queen simultaneously triumphing over but also sensually and analogously part of the sea and the land of her kingdom.

Whatever the future status promised to her by Prospero, while she is on the island Miranda is very far from exercising power. If her class position gives her authority over Caliban, her gender dramatically undercuts that power by making her frighteningly vulnerable to his attempted act of rape – a vulnerability that is even further underscored when Prospero imagines the same threat as present not only in savage but also in civilised males, and in no uncertain terms warns Ferdinand off any premature attempts to consummate the marriage. Miranda's femaleness renders her, too, the subject of her father. The man who has lost his dukedom through neglect

[21]For brief but suggestive commentary on this debate – which is all the more intriguing since *The Tempest* in general is such a clean text – see Michael Hattaway, 'Drama and society', in *The Cambridge Companion to English Renaissance Drama*, edited by A. R. Braunmuller and Michael Hattaway (Cambridge: Cambridge University Press, 1990), p. 120. Hattaway asks, 'Do we hear the accents of Miranda in Caliban's "poetical" speeches? Does Prospero wish to suppress women's language?'

clearly has no intention of allowing history to repeat itself with his daughter: her attention is constantly enjoined; her wish not to see Caliban – ''Tis a villain, sir,/I do not love to look on' (I.ii.310–11) – is ignored; her access to knowledge and even to consciousness is controlled by her father's insistent shielding of Ariel's presence from her and by his deployment of enchanted sleeps to keep information from her. Indeed, the extent to which her thought processes have effectively been colonised by Prospero is clearly illustrated by her confident declaration that 'Good wombs have borne bad sons' (I.ii.120); her pronouncement is made on an area in which she can have no knowledge, expressing an opinion moulded entirely by her father.[22]

Miranda is not, however, quite so passive a receptacle for Prospero's educational processes as he might like to think. Like Caliban, whose own speech and thought processes still visibly underlie the veneer of civilisation which has been foisted upon him, Miranda still retains residual elements of a consciousness not moulded entirely to Prospero's will. To her father's confident assumption that she will have no memory preceding their arrival upon the island, she ripostes that she does indeed have a recollection, which is, interestingly enough, of the company of other women – 'Had I not/Four or five women once, that tended me?' (I.ii.46–7) – and despite Prospero's careful description of their mutual enemies, she refuses to demonise Ferdinand as one of those 'Others' whom Prospero's language has so carefully constructed for her. In this she is, of course, proceeding in accordance with

[22] For comment on this passage, see for instance Ann Thompson, '"Miranda, where's your sister?": Reading Shakespeare's *The Tempest*', in *Feminist Criticism: Theory and Practice*, edited by Susan Sellers (Hemel Hempstead: Harvester Wheatsheaf, 1991), pp. 45–55, p. 46.

Prospero's ultimate plan; but he – and we – may nevertheless still be surprised at how quickly, after 12 years of tête-à-tête, she shakes off his tutelage.

The admired Miranda has in fact gone through a precise volte-face. Refusing to be constructed as a passive object of admiration, she impatiently dismisses Ferdinand's praises and raptures and concentrates, instead, on admiring *him* – and, in due course, his countrymen. It certainly seems significant that the remark for which Miranda has always been most famous is 'O brave new world/That has such people in't' (V.i.183–4); here the admired one turns the tables, admiring back; the classified, labelled female applies a label of her own, expropriating Adam's privilege of naming all new kinds and simultaneously constructing man, not woman, as a new world, open for colonisation. Prospero's cynical response, ''Tis new to thee' (V.i.184), misses a large part of the point: of course it is new to her, but that does not automatically mean she can't provide an intelligent response to it, for what she sees will be neither so unfamiliar as to disable all categories of recognition, nor so hackneyed as to prevent a fresh assessment. What we are offered here is a returning of the gaze; a reversal of the power structures habitually present in the colonising act of looking on as the passive, admired one exercises the active function of admiration. It is, above all, in this characteristically Shakespearean ability to imagine a visual turning of the tables – to register not only how the 'natives' look to us, but also how *we* may look to *them* – that *The Tempest* negotiates much the same answer to the English colonial enterprise as does the Strachey source text.

Miranda's admiring gaze serves also to reinforce the play's insistence on the subjectivity of all forms of perception, as when the Neapolitan lords all see such very different islands in Act II, scene i:

ADRIAN

The air breathes upon us here most sweetly.

SEBASTIAN

As if it had lungs, and rotten ones.

ANTONIO

Or, as 'twere perfumed by a fen.

GONZALO

Here is everything advantageous to life.

ANTONIO

True, save means to live.

(II.i.49–53)

The Shakespearean stage had few props and no scenery, and therefore inevitably depended heavily on characters' verbal descriptions to inform the audience of where they were and what it looked like. It is very unusual for different characters to describe the same scene in different ways: perhaps the only other example is in the Dover Cliff scene of *King Lear* – and there, one character is blind and the other deliberately trying to deceive him about the nature of the landscape. The effect of this scene for Shakespeare's original audience would, therefore, be particularly striking.

However the characters see the island, though, one thing is certain: everyone wants to rule it. This is an indication of another prominent concern in the play: its interest in ideas of Utopia. When Gonzalo says 'Had I plantation of this isle, my lord' (II.i.144), he introduces a major Renaissance theme, first explored in Sir Thomas More's *Utopia* and ironically developed in the following exchange from *The Tempest*:

GONZALO

I'th'commonwealth I would by contraries
Execute all things, for no kind of traffic
Would I admit; no name of magistrate;
Letters should not be known; riches, poverty
And use of service, none; contract, succession,
Bourn, bound of land, tilth, vineyard – none;
No use of metal, corn, or wine or oil;
No occupation, all men idle, all;
And women, too, but innocent and pure;
No sovereignty –

SEBASTIAN

                Yet he would be king on't.

                      (II.i.148–157)

As David J. Baker points out, 'The authority of kingship is in question from the opening scene of The Tempest',[23] where the Boatswain asks scornfully 'What cares these roarers for the name of king?' (I.i.16–17), and yet it seems impossible for 'the good Gonzalo' to imagine any other political system.

    This may remind us that texts dealing with colonialism often constitute themselves as sites for the examination of the merits and demerits of various forms of government. This is certainly the case in many of the weighty theologico-legal tracts produced in support or condemnation of the Spanish kings' right to the Indies: the Spanish writers las Casas, Mendieta, and Sepulveda all consider the Indians' right to self-rule not only in isolation, but also as a test case of that fundamental Renaissance concept, Natural Law, which

---

[23] Baker, 'Where is Ireland in The Tempest?', p. 72.

co-exists so problematically with civic and secular rule.[24] A similar connection is made, too, in that most famous of all linkings of women and colonialism, John Donne's 'Elegy 19', where the process of exploring a new country is seen principally in terms of the way in which it should be ruled:

O my America, my new-found land
My kingdom, safeliest when with one man manned.

In Donne as in The Tempest, and in many other colonial texts, the European system is examined only to be endorsed: the king is taken as the emblem of good government. In Donne's poem, this cultural and social preference is glossed as natural by the implicit comparison to 'normal', 'natural' relationships between men and women. Similarly in The Tempest, the idea of a ruling woman – such as Sycorax was, or such as both Claribel and Miranda briefly threatened to be – is raised only to be safely dismissed to the margins of the text. As Ania Loomba points out, 'Prospero as colonialist consolidates power which is specifically white and male'.[25] As we will see, this is also something which will be accepted as natural in many, though not quite all, screen adaptations of the play.

[24] See Englander et al, Culture and Belief, pp. 321–38.

[25] Ania Loomba, Gender, Race, Renaissance Drama (Manchester: Manchester University Press, 1989), p. 152.

the play today

∙∙∙

Colonialism, Utopia and theories of government were all important Renaissance concerns and motifs, but time has brought with it other ways of reading the The Tempest.

Two or three years ago, when I was teaching the play to a group of final-year undergraduates, one of them said, 'This is exactly like The Fight Club.' I duly rented and watched The Fight Club and concluded that it was not remotely like The Tempest. When I told the student so, he explained that he had taken Ariel and Caliban to be not real characters, but rather emanations of Prospero's psyche – as the Brad Pitt character in The Fight Club is of the narrator's. This is a reading that the play would seem to go some way towards supporting. It is certainly possible to read Ariel and Caliban as functioning along the lines of the superego and the id, and it is notable that it is only Prospero who ever sees Ariel in his 'normal' guise. Equally, as Alden T. Vaughan and Virginia Mason Vaughan point out, Caliban 'never appears on stage with either Ariel or Ferdinand. He presumably does not know of Ferdinand at all, and he may be oblivious to Ariel's existence';[26] so too may

[26] Alden T. Vaughan and Virginia Mason Vaughan, Shakespeare's Caliban: A Cultural History (Cambridge: Cambridge University Press, 1991), p. 16.

Miranda, who never interacts with or shows any awareness of Ariel. This extreme isolation of characters from each other contributes to the impression of events as locked in individual characters' heads rather than communally experienced, as too does the fact, already discussed, that individuals all view the island in such different ways. Indeed, Prospero seems openly to draw attention to the possibility of a psychologised reading of physical locations when he speaks of the human mind as if it were the shore of a sea:

> Their understanding
> Begins to swell, and the approaching tide
> Will shortly fill the reasonable shore
> That now lies foul and muddy.
>
> (V.i. 79–82)

Is the island of *The Tempest*, then, a real, material island or a metaphor for the psyche?

There are other approaches and questions which modern critics have found it useful to apply to *The Tempest*. One important consideration is genre. *The Tempest* is generally termed a 'last play' or 'late romance' – a uniquely Shakespearean genre comprising *The Tempest*, *The Winter's Tale*, *Cymbeline* and *Pericles*, all of which focus on father/daughter relationships, sea voyages, and family losses and reunions. Certainly Miranda's name – like those of the other heroines in Shakespeare's last plays – is unusual in the marked extent to which it offers not only a label, but also a reading of its possessor. Imogen in *Cymbeline* should more properly be Innogen, 'born from the deep', and so shares her etymology with the sea-born Marina in *Pericles*; Perdita in *The Winter's Tale* is, of course, lost. (Amongst the other heroines, only *Hamlet*'s Ophelia, whose name could ironically be transliterated to form the Greek for 'help', demonstrates a similar phenomenon.) This use of names gives the play an allegorical feel, and indeed all the last plays feature strange, dreamlike events and an interest in magic and miracles, taking them a long way away from any kind of realist aesthetic and seeming to position them very firmly as romances, in the classic sense of fantastic narratives which often involve exotic voyages and miraculous or near-miraculous events.

However, this is not the only genre to which *The Tempest* could be assigned. Dan DeWeese argues that the play 'examines what life a *pharmakos* might expect to lead after being expelled from the city'.[27] *Pharmakos* is the Greek word for a scapegoat, a sacrificial animal onto whose back the sins of the entire community are loaded and which suffers so that others need not. This would make the play a classic exploration of tragedy – a word supposed to derive originally from the Greek 'tragoidia', or 'goatsong' (presumed to refer in this context to the idea of the scapegoat). In Paul Mazursky's 1982 film of *The Tempest*, Phillip Dimitrius, the Prospero figure (John Cassavetes), kills a goat for a feast, which might well seem to signal such an understanding of the narrative, especially since it is clear that his aggression against the goat is a reflection of that which he might otherwise have shown against those who have betrayed him. However, in the First Folio of Shakespeare's plays *The Tempest* appeared among the comedies, and Russell Jackson's discussion of Derek Jarman's film of *The Tempest* is to be found in a chapter on 'Shakespeare's Comedies

[27] Dan DeWeese, 'Prospero's Pharmacy: Peter Greenaway and the Critics Play Shakespeare's Mimetic Game', in *Almost Shakespeare: Reinventing his Works for Cinema and Television*, edited by James R. Keller and Leslie Stratyner (Jefferson, NC: McFarland and Company, 2004), pp. 155–168, p. 156.

on Film'.[28] The genre of *The Tempest* is, it seems, territory almost as disputed as the play's fictional island.

It also needs to be noted that *The Tempest* makes explicit reference to yet another, very specific, genre: the masque. Many of Shakespeare's plays contain a play-within-the-play; *The Tempest*, uniquely, contains a masque-within-the-play. Masques are different from plays in that they are associated with a courtly rather than a popular audience – and indeed with courtly performers as well, since they were put on at court with the queen, Anne of Denmark, herself taking a leading rôle. When Prospero has Ariel and his fellow sprites 'present' Ceres, Iris and Juno, the contemporary audience would immediately have recognised this as a masque, in which the 'real' identities of the performers were intended to be clearly obvious (thus Ariel openly refers to the fact that he played Ceres (IV.i.167)).

As well as genre-based approaches to the play, other, very different interpretations are possible. In his Oxford edition of the play, Stephen Orgel includes in the introduction the following sections: 'The Renaissance Political Context', with subheadings on 'Political Marriages', 'Utopia and the New World', and 'Authority'; 'Epic and History', with a subheading on 'Italy and Carthage'; and 'The Masque', with a subheading on 'The Masque as Image and Symbol'. The volume includes appendices on 'The Seamanship of Act I, Scene I', 'The Strachey Letter', 'The Music', 'Florio's Montaigne', and 'Medea's Incantation'.[29] In their edition for the Arden 3 series,

---

[28] Russell Jackson, 'Shakespeare's Comedies on Film', in *Shakespeare and the Moving Image: The Plays on Film and Television*, edited by Anthony Davies and Stanley Wells (Cambridge: Cambridge University Press, 1994), pp. 99–120.

[29] William Shakespeare, *The Tempest*, edited by Stephen Orgel (Oxford: Oxford University Press, 1994).

Virginia Mason Vaughan and Alden T. Vaughan include in the introduction a section on 'Context', which includes subheadings on 'Domestic Politics', 'Brave New World', 'Africa and Ireland', 'Literary Forerunners', 'Classical Models', 'The "Salvage Man"', 'Magic' and 'Masque'. There are also two appendices: the first is on 'Sources' and includes the Strachey Letter and Montaigne's 'Of the Caniballes'; the second is on 'Appropriations' and includes Browning's 'Caliban upon Setebos', Rodó's 'Ariel', and Mannoni on Prospero and Caliban. In both these editions, it is clear that *The Tempest* is a play which can be seen with equal ease as reaching both deep into the past ('Epic and History', 'Italy and Carthage') and far into the future ('Africa and Ireland', 'Appropriations').

It is, therefore, unsurprising that one aspect of the play has proved to be of considerable interest to critics: its obsession with time, and the associated idea of place. As has often been observed by critics, *The Tempest*, Shakespeare's last play, is one of only two of Shakespeare's plays to observe the Aristotelian unities of time, place, and action (the other is *The Comedy of Errors*, which was almost certainly his first); yet at the same time as it ostensibly obeys the unities, it also and at the same time subverts them. Although the action of the play covers only one day, the play insistently remembers the past, and in particular the classical past: the work of Margaret Tudeau-Clayton and others has shown the enormous importance of Virgil's *Aeneid* to this play.[30] The first words of Ferdinand to Miranda, 'Most sure, the goddess', echo those of Aeneas to the first female he meets in Africa, 'O dea certe', and we are explicitly told that 'This Tunis, sir, was Carthage' (II.i.84), the city where Aeneas met Dido. Moreover, Alden T. Vaughan and

---

[30] Margaret Tudeau-Clayton, *Jonson, Shakespeare, and Early Modern Virgil* (Cambridge: Cambridge University Press, 1998).

Virginia Mason Vaughan compare Caliban to Polyphemus, the Cyclops in another epic, the *Odyssey*.[31] At the same time, however, *The Tempest* has inspired several notable retellings set in a far-off future.

Equally, although the play is set all in one place, it proves to be a place that is impossible to identify with any certainty: not only is the whole point of a Utopia (literally 'no place' in Greek) that it has no identifiable geographical location, but the play itself insistently suggests both a location in the Caribbean and one in the Mediterranean. As Jerry Brotton points out,

> The presence of a more definable Mediterranean geography which runs throughout the play, and which emanates outwards from the disputation over contemporary Tunis and classical Carthage, suggests that *The Tempest* is much more of a politically and geographically bifurcated play in the negotiation between its Mediterranean and Atlantic contexts than critics have recently been prepared to concede.[32]

The much-commented-on reference to the 'still-vexed Bermudas' (I.ii.229) gives both an anchor point and, simultaneously and paradoxically, a place where the inhabitants of the island are *not*, since the Bermudas are somewhere to which Ariel will have to go. It has, moreover, been repeatedly suggested that the concerns of *The Tempest* were in fact much closer to home: David J. Baker argues that *The Tempest* is about 'a dynamic relation *between*

---

[31] Vaughan and Vaughan, *Shakespeare's Caliban*, p. 58.

[32] Jerry Brotton, '"This Tunis, sir, was Carthage": Contesting colonialism in *The Tempest*', in *Post-Colonial Shakespeares*, edited by Ania Loomba and Martin Orkin (London: Routledge, 1998), pp. 23–42, p. 24.

places on the globe that Shakespeare knew: America, England, and Ireland'.[33] It is little wonder that adaptations of the play have chosen such diverse settings as the Mississippi bayous, a Greek island, and the fictional planet Altair IV.

---

[33] David J. Baker, 'Where is Ireland in *The Tempest*?', in *Shakespeare and Ireland: History, Politics, Culture*, edited by Mark Thornton Burnett and Ramona Wray (Basingstoke: Macmillan, 1997), pp. 68–88, p. 69.

the tempest – a brief overview

Few plays have been more frequently or more extensively adapted than *The Tempest*. It has spawned a host of novelisations, poems, and plays as well as inspiring essays and polemics. Very often the changes made have had the intention (or at least the effect) of pressing the text into the services of arguments for or against colonialism. As Susan Bennett points out, 'Caliban in the last 150 years has been represented as an Australian aboriginal, an American Indian, a West Indian, an Indian, an African, a Boer, a "red republican", a "missing link", a "Hun", and an Irishman'.[34] Indeed, Caliban has effectively taken on a life of his own: Ruth Morse speaks of him as 'a little like a planetary moon which has escaped its orbit to become a new centre',[35] and Nadia Lie and Theo D'haen observe,

> In "Calibán," an essay published in the early 1970s, the Cuban critic Roberto Fernández Retamar launched an appeal to

---

[34] Bennett, *Performing Nostalgia*, p. 124.
[35] Ruth Morse, 'Monsters, Magiçians, Movies: *The Tempest* and the Final Frontier', *Shakespeare Survey* 53 (2000), pp. 164–174, p. 165.

consider literature and history not just from the point of view of Prospero, but also from that of Caliban ... The subsequent publication of two major studies wholly devoted to Caliban – Alden T. Vaughan and Virginia Mason Vaughan's 1991 *Shakespeare's Caliban: A Cultural History*, and the 1992 *Caliban* volume in the Chelsea House *Major Literary Characters* series – bears out the degree to which literary and cultural studies have taken these appeals seriously. In fact, a whole new discipline seems to have emerged: "Calibanology."[36]

Edmond Malone observed that Caliban's costume in the 18th century, 'which doubtless was originally prescribed by the poet himself and has been continued, I believe, since his time, is a large bear skin, or the skin of some other animal; and he is usually presented with long shaggy hair'.[37] For Malone and the century which followed him, then, Caliban was little more than an animal, and this was a play that was always about Prospero; but for the 20th and 21st centuries, it has become as often as not about Caliban.

This emphasis on Caliban has in turn inflected dominant critical approaches to the play. Aimé Césaire's *Une Tempête*, Marina Warner's *Indigo*, and numerous other reworkings have all constituted *The Tempest* as a key text for discussion of issues associated not only with the originary moment of colonialism, but also with what it was subsequently to become. As Jonathan Hart observes,

[36] Nadia Lie and Theo D'haen, eds, *Constellation Caliban: Figurations of a Character* (Amsterdam: Rodopi, 1997), preface, p. i.
[37] Rowland Wymer, 'The Tempest and the Origins of Britain', *Critical Survey* 11.1 (1999), pp. 3–14, p. 7.

Between 1957 and 1973, most African and large Caribbean colonies won their independence. Dissenting intellectuals and writers from these regions decided to appropriate *The Tempest* as a means of supporting decolonization and creating an alternative literary tradition ... For 40 years or more – in Spanish, French and English – African and Caribbean writers and critics have, directly and indirectly, appropriated or discussed the appropriation of Shakespeare's play. For instance, in 1969 Aimé Césaire's *Une Tempête: D'après "la Tempête" de Shakespeare – Adaptation pour un théâtre nègre* was published in Paris ... in "Calypso for Caliban", which is in *Highlife for Caliban*, Lemuel Johnson shows what Caliban has done with Prospero's language, life and history: "papa prospero/jig me mama".[38]

Nor did the use of *The Tempest* stop there:

Sustained encounters with *The Tempest* are recorded in a host of imaginative and theoretical texts of the postwar decades of national emergence, beginning with Octave Mannoni's *Psychology of Colonization* (1950) and Frantz Fanon's *Black Skin, White Masks* (1952), and notably including George Lamming's *The Pleasures of Exile* (1960) and *Water with Berries* (1971), Aimé Césaire's *A Tempest* (1969), Roberto Fernández Retamar's *Caliban* (1971), and *A Grain of Wheat* (1968), among other works, by the Kenyan Ngugi wa Thiong'o. In most of these works, contemporaneous British and American attempts to problem-atize the traditionally stereotyped critical estimate of the relationship of Prospero and Caliban are resisted in favor of

[38] Jonathan Hart, *Columbus, Shakespeare, and the Interpretation of the New World* (New York: Palgrave, 2003), p. 130.

recuperating the starkness of the master/slave configuration, thus making it appear to function as a foundational paradigm in the history of European colonialism. In this process, writers like Ngugi, Lamming, and Césaire regenerate out of their own firsthand experience of colonization a conception of Shakespeare as a formative producer and purveyor of a paternalistic ideology that is basic to the material aims of Western imperialism.[39]

It is little wonder, then, that so much recent criticism has approached the play from this angle. In Peter Childs' *Post-Colonial Theory and English Literature: A Reader*, for instance, there are four separate pieces on *The Tempest* (they are, respectively, extracts from Trevor R. Griffiths, '"This Island's Mine": Caliban and Colonialism', Rob Nixon, 'Caribbean and African Appropriations of *The Tempest*'; Meredith Anne Skura, 'Discourse and the Individual: The Case of Colonialism in *The Tempest*'; and Sylvia Wynter, 'Beyond Miranda's Meanings: Un/silencing the "Demonic Ground" of Caliban's "Woman"').

Despite the play's interest in the past, it has often been adapted as or formed the basis for an allegory of the future, perhaps most notably in Aldous Huxley's *Brave New World* (first published in 1932), where genetic engineering triumphs in a world in which Shakespeare is outlawed, and in which John's Savage plays an ironic Caliban to Lenina's lustful Miranda. Particularly after Darwin, the play has also been increasingly understood as raising the issue of the relationship between humans and animals. Darwinian ideas had a profound impact on the understanding and staging of two

[39] Thomas Cartelli, *Repositioning Shakespeare: National formations, postcolonial appropriations* (London: Routledge, 1999), p. 89.

Shakespeare plays in particular, *Othello* and *The Tempest*. *The Tempest* had already figured prominently in the earlier history of literature associated with scientific progress: Jane Blumberg suggests that when Mary Shelley was writing *Frankenstein*, in which an indebtedness to the theories of Darwin's proto-evolutionist grandfather Erasmus is explicitly acknowledged, her reading of *The Tempest* at around the same time may have led her to conceive Victor Frankenstein and the creature he makes partly in terms of Ariel and Caliban.[40] Certainly the two texts were later to be virtually conflated in the many Victorian cartoons to depict the Irish as either O'Frankensteins or as Caliban figures.[41] Indeed, Caliban became a versatile emblem for all sorts of alleged subhumanity, as in J. Compton Rickett's *The Quickening of Caliban* (1893), in which a living 'missing link' is found; while the title of Daniel Wilson's *Caliban: The Missing Link* (1897) states its thesis even more bluntly, before going on to argue that Shakespeare, 'in the Caliban of his "Tempest", anticipates and satisfies the most startling problem of the 19th century':

> It will need no apology to the appreciative student of Shake-speare that "the missing link" in the evolution of man should be sought for in the pages of him "whose aim was to hold as 'twere the mirror up to nature;" nor, if it is to be recovered anywhere, will he wonder at its discovery there.[42]

---

[40] Jane Blumberg, *Mary Shelley's Early Novels* (Basingstoke: Macmillan, 1993), p. 42.

[41] L. Perry Curtis, Jr, *Apes and Angels: The Irishmen in Victorian Caricature* (Newton Abbot: David & Charles, 1971), pp. 22 and 45.

[42] Daniel Wilson, *Caliban: The Missing Link* (London: Macmillan, 1873), p. 192 and Preface, p. viii.

Wilson speculates that modern man himself may be to the man of the future as Caliban is to Prospero,[43] and in H. G. Wells' *The Time Traveller* (1895) the eponymous hero wonders whether he may not himself be the Caliban to the Eloi Weena's Ariel – an inversion of customary polarities that is echoed in Bram Stoker's *The Lady of the Shroud* (1909), where the Irish-born hero Rupert Sent Leger calls his degenerate English cousin 'a modern Caliban' who cannot compete against the fitter Balkan-born Men of the Blue Mountains.[44] This evolutionary understanding of Caliban is, I shall be suggesting, a hidden presence in Percy Stow's 1908 screen adaptation, and an interest in Darwin is also a pervasive concern throughout Greenaway's *oeuvre*;[45] indeed, John Orr comments on Greenaway's 'desire to be a new Darwin, to adopt the Victorian genus of natural selection as his own double and as a metaphor of omnipotent filmmaking'.[46] Most notably, when Alonso in Mazursky's *Tempest* asks 'Who's Kalibanos?', Phillip replies, 'Your long-lost ancestor', although Kalibanos is also termed 'a fish in drag' and there is a scene in which Miranda, watching TV, has Kalibanos on one side and a goat on the other; when he speaks, it bleats. In this wildly versatile play, then, Caliban has proved the most versatile character of all.

Issues for adaptation

- **Setting**. The Neapolitans in *The Tempest* are on their way home to Naples from Tunis. They ought, therefore, to be in the Mediter-

[43] Wilson, *Caliban*, pp. 119–20.

[44] Bram Stoker, *The Lady of the Shroud* [1909] (London: Alan Sutton, 1994), p. 207.

[45] See Alan Woods, *Being Naked Playing Dead: The Art of Peter Greenaway* (Manchester: Manchester University Press, 1996), pp. 17 and 64ff.

[46] John Orr, 'The Art of National Identity: Peter Greenaway and Derek Jarman', in *British Cinema, Past and Present*, edited by Justine Ashby and Andrew Higson (London: Routledge, 2000), pp. 327–338, p. 336.

ranean. But the play's main source was an account of a shipwreck in the North Atlantic; it has been much adapted in the Caribbean, Africa, and India; it makes extensive use of classical mythology; and recent critics have linked it increasingly to Ireland. The choice of where to set any adaptation of the play is therefore a particularly loaded one. Moreover, setting also influences questions of visual style, especially if Alden T. Vaughan and Virginia Mason Vaughan are right to think that 'As one of Shakespeare's most unrealistic plays, *The Tempest* is not suited to Zeffirelli's evocations of local color or Peter Brook's harsh documentary style'.[47] What then should Prospero's island look like; and what, if anything, can or should a director do about the fact that different characters see it in different ways?

- **Timeframe.** To a Renaissance audience, *The Tempest*, with its classicising masque and Virgilian allusions, would have appeared to be ostentatiously advertising its grounding in the classical past. More recently, however, it has been most often understood as an allegory of the future. Choice of period is therefore a crucial issue.
- **Genre.** Should the story be understood as comedy, tragedy, romance, or perhaps as science fiction?
- **How 'brave' is the 'new world'?** When the Europeans land on the island, each of them sees it differently; in turn, when Miranda and Prospero look at the Europeans, she is impressed while he is not. Since Aldous Huxley, it is almost impossible not to hear irony in the phrase 'brave new world'. How then should film audiences be invited to judge the tone of the end of the narrative?
- What should a director do with **the masque**, a form with which no modern audience will be familiar?
- Who or what are **Caliban and Ariel**?

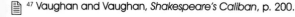 [47] Vaughan and Vaughan, *Shakespeare's Caliban*, p. 200.

- What should be done with Prospero's long account to Miranda of the `backstory`?
- Can film do better than the stage with the elements of **magic** in the play?
- **Music** plays an important part in *The Tempest*; Caliban says `The isle is full of noises' (III.iii.135), and John P. Cutts declares that `the whole play is conceived as taking part on an island that resounds continually to music in the air, which is, I believe, equivalent to the music of the spheres'.[48] Film has often found music particularly congenial to its purposes, for highlighting atmosphere and signalling narrative climaxes and also for indicating and developing character. What then is the rôle of music in a music-friendly medium's adaptation of a music-rich play?
- Miranda's name identifies her as a classic object of the gaze, but she also exercises the privilege of gazing. To what extent do the cameras of the various directors treated here dwell on **Miranda**?

In the sections that follow, I will be looking at a variety of adaptations in the light of these and other questions.

[48] John P. Cutts, `Music and the Supernatural in *The Tempest*', in *Shakespeare*, The Tempest: *A Casebook*, edited by D. J. Palmer (Basingstoke: Macmillan, 1968), pp. 196–211, p. 196.

PART TWO

From text to screen

introduction – setting the scene

The main focus of this book is on the three most celebrated screen adapations of *The Tempest*: **Forbidden Planet (1956)**; **Derek Jarman's 1979 film, *The Tempest***; and **Peter Greenaway's *Prospero's Books* (1991)**. However, in order to contextualise these it is important first to set the scene by looking at the general history of screen adaptations of the play.

Although the first film version of *The Tempest* appears to date from 1905, it is now lost and little is known of it.[1] The history of adaptation of *The Tempest* thus effectively begins in 1908, with Percy Stow's 12-minute silent version of the play. This was made by the Clarendon Film Company (cast unknown), and released in 1999 as part of the BFI video *Silent Shakespeare*. Perforce both silent and in black and white, the film focuses principally on the backstory. The first four scenes all cover events which occurred before the play starts, and much is omitted: in particular, neither Stephano nor Trinculo appears, so there is no treason plot against Prospero and also no comedy. The film assumes strong knowledge of the text,

[1] Alden T. Vaughan and Virginia Mason Vaughan, *Shakespeare's Caliban: A Cultural History* (Cambridge: Cambridge University Press, 1991), p. 201.

and indeed would hardly be comprehensible without it; in fact it bears something of the same relationship to Shakespeare's play as a piece of music inspired by it might. It stresses principally the magic of the play – Ariel transforms herself (in this case) into a cat on camera – but does offer some other noteworthy features: John P. McCombe calls it a 'transitional film' between what Tom Gunning termed 'the cinema of attraction' and 'the narrator system',[2] and both these aspects of the film are worth attention.

It is particularly striking that Caliban offers no provocation to Prospero before being caught – he is seen as fair game (a suggestion underlined by the fact that he is literally close to the earth, as if he were indeed a game bird or animal) and Prospero virtually stalks him (after having apparently taken quite some time to find him, judging by how much longer his beard is than when he landed). In the context of the period, this is immensely significant. Stow's film was made in the same year that Baden-Powell's *Scouting for Boys*, which included a section on 'Men's Tracks', was published.[3] In the wake of the publication of Edwin Ray Lankester's *Degeneration: A Chapter in Darwinism* (1880), the alarming revelations about the physical unfitness of many of the troops conscripted for the Boer War, and above all the trial of Oscar Wilde, Baden-Powell aimed to redress what he saw as the degeneration of Englishmen by inculcating survival skills, particularly those of hunting and tracking. (There is a modern parallel in *The Simpsons*, when Homer fears that Marge's gay friend may turn Bart gay too;

[2] John P. McCombe, '"Suiting the Action to the Word": The Clarendon *Tempest* and the Evolution of a Narrative Silent Shakespeare', *Literature/Film Quarterly* 33.2 (2005), pp. 142–155, p. 142.

[3] Robert Baden-Powell, *Scouting for Boys*, edited by Elleke Boehmer (Oxford: Oxford University Press, 2004), pp. 77 ff.

Mo advises him to take Bart hunting on the grounds that 'After the boy bags a deer, all the diet Sodas in the world won't turn him back'.) For the Victorians and the Edwardians, hunting was not merely recreation; it was simultaneously a form of 'species policing' and of asserting a radical difference between man and animals. In Stow's film, the iconography of this first encounter between Prospero and Caliban would therefore have been clear: Prospero is fully human, and concomitantly fully superior; Caliban is, as he was for Malone in the 18th century, effectively an animal, and as such Prospero's legitimate prey. This idea will later be interestingly revisited in *Forbidden Planet*, where, as Simone Caroti points out, tracking and detection come to the fore again as 'Footprints and energy signatures are examined'.[4]

Unlike *Forbidden Planet*, though, Stow's film is entirely confident in the polarities of the relationships it depicts: Caliban is bad, and Prospero is good, and there is not even the faintest possibility of any relationship between the two. So, far from there being any suggestion that Prospero might be to blame for his treatment of Caliban, and must learn to accept a form of kinship between them, Caliban simply disappears from the story. Prospero's long white beard makes him look like a cross between a judge and Father Christmas; his hairstyle resembles a judge's wig, implying good judgement, and suggestions of the godlike and of justice are reinforced by the absence of any hint of guilt or negligence attached to his exile – the caption tells us merely that 'Prospero seeks refuge on an island', and the closing caption which bookends this – 'Friends Once More' – suggests that a simple quarrel had

[4] Simone Caroti, 'Science Fiction, *Forbidden Planet*, and Shakespeare's *The Tempest*', *Comparative Literature and Culture* 6.1 (March, 2004). Online: http://clcwebjournal.lib.purdue.edu/clcweb04-1/caroti04.html

been the cause of his flight. Prospero's status is also enhanced by the Christian purpose implied in the caption 'To humble Prince Ferdinand, Prospero sets him to log shifting', and by the fact that he raises his hands to heaven when he first sees Miranda and Ferdinand together. Moreover, the doves that Prospero produces before the storm could be seen as alluding to the story of Noah.

In keeping with the wisdom and benevolence posited for Prospero, Miranda here is virginal and innocent, as indicated by the fact that she is dressed entirely in white. Unlike the Miranda of the play, she is also allowed to see Ariel, who is presented in the film as an ageless young girl and thus a perfectly proper companion; indeed, in what we shall see is a recurring feature of film adaptations of the play, there is a bond implied between Ariel and Miranda – Ferdinand follows Ariel to find Miranda, and it is Ariel, not Prospero, who rescues her from Caliban. There is, however, no real sense of a threat from Caliban or anyone else, because all the villains are funny rather than menacing: not only are their gestures inevitably jerky, but they are comically swamped by their costumes (to a modern audience, Caliban looks strikingly like Robbie Coltrane's Hagrid). Finally, the production is taken completely out of time when they all sail off in a longship with a dragon figurehead, an image which completely disables any possibility of relating the events to any contemporary issues.

Since this first surviving film, and a silent 1911 American film which is now lost but 'was particularly commended for its exquisite storm effects',[5] there have been at least 15 filmed versions of *The Tempest*. Notable adaptations include a 1939 black-and-white version directed by Dallas Bower and starring a young Peggy Ashcroft as Miranda and the horror actor Dennis Price as the ship's master, and

[5] Judith Buchanan, *Shakespeare on Film* (Longman: Pearson, 2005), p. 43.

a 1989 Swedish-language cartoon version called *Resan till Melonia*, directed by Per Åhlin and featuring in its cast a character called Captain Christmas Tree. As Judith Buchanan points out, there was also at least one version that went unmade: from 1969 to 1979 Michael Powell made intermittent attempts to film a version of *The Tempest* which would have starred James Mason as Prospero and, at one stage, Mia Farrow as Ariel. This would have been virtually unique in finding Caliban more sympathetic than Prospero, and would have been explicitly set inside Prospero's head.[6]

There are also shades of *The Tempest* in at least one film which may at first glance seem a long way removed from the play. In a neat returning of the compliment of influence, Disney's *Pocahontas* (directed by Mike Gabriel and Eric Goldberg, in 1995) can be seen as echoing *The Tempest*. As soon as the ship sails we encounter a terrific storm in which a lot of nautical instructions are shouted, and Governor Ratcliffe echoes some of the key terms of Shakespeare's play when he declares: 'It won't be long before we reach the New World, and remember what awaits us there – freedom, prosperity.' This is the first of many uses in which the term 'New World' is increasingly ironised. Grandmother Willow speaking from a tree may recall Ariel locked in the cloven pine, and Pocahontas, like Miranda, is a 'native' who returns the gaze. Most notably, the film seems to glance at *The Tempest* when it so summarily disposes of the language barrier, since John Smith might well share Ferdinand's surprise at hearing 'My language!' spoken by a woman in a far-distant land.

Like *Pocahontas*, several of the adaptations of *The Tempest* have been marked by the degree of their divergence from the events of the play. Tony Howard identifies a Western version in

[6] Buchanan, *Shakespeare on Film*, pp. 157 ff.

Yellow Sky (directed by William A. Wellman, in 1949),[7] in which an unnamed old man (James Barton) who is a 'prospector' is the Prospero figure, and his granddaughter 'Mike' (real name Constance Mae, played by Anne Baxter) is Miranda – although the way in which she tells the incomers to find water and is often seen performing domestic tasks also has echoes of Caliban, and the way in which her presence sets the men at odds with each other foreshadows *Forbidden Planet* rather than echoing *The Tempest* (moreover, gold is their secret, as the Krell laboratory is Morbius's). There is, however, no Caliban nor Ariel, unless the Apaches can be seen as having a function in this respect: we are told by her grandfather that Mike has been raised by Apaches, though this is never confirmed and no explanation is offered of why it should be so, and they do at one point provide an apparent promise of rescue. However, it is true that the film opens in a storm, while the yellow sky of the title – a ghost town; the film was shot partly here and partly in Death Valley – could echo *The Tempest*'s yellow sands. Moreover, when 'Stretch' twice tells his men that he doesn't like votes, and intends to wield power regardless of their opinion, the government theme of *The Tempest* is evoked. On the whole, though, the differences between *Yellow Sky* and *The Tempest* are more strongly marked than are the similarities.

Other adaptations, by contrast, have stayed stultifyingly close to the original text. Most notable in this latter respect – as was typical of the series as a whole – was the BBC Shakespeare version of the play, directed by John Gorrie in 1980. This had a wealth of acting talent, including Michael Hordern as Prospero, Warren

---

[7] Tony Howard, 'Shakespeare's Cinematic Offshoots', in *The Cambridge Companion to Shakespeare on Film*, edited by Russell Jackson (Cambridge: Cambridge University Press, 2000), pp. 295–313, p. 306.

Clarke as Caliban, Nigel Hawthorne as Stephano and Andrew Sachs as Trinculo, but was leaden and undistinguished and entirely devoid of invention, being, as Deborah Cartmell aptly terms it, 'a simple, undemanding reading of the play'.[8] The nearest we come to a display of the powers of television is when Ariel (David Dixon of Ford Prefect fame from *The Hitchhiker's Guide to the Galaxy*) jumps into the air and disappears; apart from that, there is no attempt to engage with the medium. No one ever looks at the camera until the epilogue, and there is some woefully unconvincing rain in the first scene. The production is very static, with all emphasis on the language. Ironically, the featureless rocks of the set and and the faintly sci-fi music make it all look a bit like *Forbidden Planet*, though it entirely lacks *Forbidden Planet*'s charm and verve; it is also set on quite an exceptionally large island, with much more of a suggestion of the planetscape than of insularity. This is a film which is strikingly conservative in its politics: Warren Clarke's excessively hairy Caliban whines and curses, removing any possibility of sympathy for him, and the only noteworthy deviation from con-ventional pieties comes from apparent homoerotic sensibility in the display of the body of Ariel, naked except for a thong, and those of the other male sprites who are present in surprising profusion (at a particularly suggestive moment, a bent sword is positioned across Ariel's crotch).

Among the more adventurous versions, Paul Mazursky's 1982 film *Tempest* is very free with the narrative. Ironically, this was not what the director originally intended: as Anthony Miller notes, 'Mazursky settled for an adaptation ... only after a prolonged attempt to plan a version that adhered to Shakespeare's text'. In the event,

---

[8] Deborah Cartmell, *Interpreting Shakespeare on Screen* (Basingstoke: Macmillan, 2000), p. 79.

'Mazursky's *Tempest* rewrites Shakespeare's play as domestic drama and as a wry reconsideration of the America that is idealised in the writings on which Shakespeare drew for his *Tempest*.[9] Among the many changes, Ariel, Antonio and Gonzalo all become female, and the island is definitively identified as Greek. Although Judith Buchanan notes that, 'Despite being voted most popular film at the Toronto Film Festival on 21 September 1982, *Tempest* was not, in general, well reviewed',[10] Douglas Bruster, situating the film within the context of Mazursky's *oeuvre* as a whole, and especially its habitual interest in infidelity, suggests that '*Tempest* is arguably the first postmodern Shakespeare film, a prologue to, even an explanation of, the many Shakespeare adaptations that followed',[11] especially when Phillip says 'We're learning how to live like human beings' and Miranda replies 'Humans go to the movies'. (There is also the fact that Mazursky and his wife have cameos.) Most recently, Paul Haspel, observing that *Tempest* is 'a motion picture so central to Mazursky's work that he titled his 1999 memoir *Show Me the Magic*, argues that

> ... both the virtues and the problems of *Tempest* stem from a discontinuity between William Shakespeare's ambiguous, unstable tragicomedy on the one hand and Mazursky's fundamentally comic and optimistic worldview on the other. Nonetheless, the film is important as a turning point for Mazursky; for in *Tempest*, he stopped restricting himself to American

[9] Anthony Miller, '"In this last tempest": Modernising Shakespeare's *Tempest* on Film', *Sydney Studies in English* 23 (1997), pp. 24–40, pp. 24 and 26.

[10] Buchanan, *Shakespeare on Film*, p. 169.

[11] Douglas Bruster, 'The Postmodern Theater of Paul Mazursky's *Tempest*', in *Shakespeare, Film, Fin-de-Siècle*, edited by Mark Thornton Burnett and Ramona Wray (Basingstoke: Macmillan, 2000), pp. 26–39, pp. 27 and 26.

characters and situations and began exploring the interaction between American culture and other cultures of the world – a creative decision that ultimately led to some of his most accomplished and successful films.[12]

Tempest takes many liberties with Shakespeare's text. Far from opening with a storm, the credits roll over perfectly calm water; the first living being seen is a goat; and the first words spoken are 'Son of a bitch'. Mazursky's Prospero figure, Phillip Dimitrius (John Cassavetes), is Greek – not an obvious choice in a period when, 20 years before *My Big Fat Greek Wedding* and *Captain Corelli's Mandolin*, mainstream cinema's image of Greece was largely confined to *Zorba the Greek* and *Never on Sunday* (the latter is indeed mentioned in Mazursky's film), especially since the Greek community in America is one of the less fully integrated, as was revealed in 1988 when Michael Dukakis stood for election as US President and was immediately portrayed as an outsider. What this unusual choice allows Mazursky to do is apply to the Old World/ New World dynamic the same sort of scrutiny as Shakespeare does in *The Tempest*, but the with the trajectory and polarities ironically reversed. Phillip is a famous New York architect in the throes of what he himself defines as a mid-life crisis: he imagines himself plunging off the top of the casino and then quits, declaring that 'The money and the power don't mean a thing'. This is hardly surprising, because all the usual New York neuroses are in evidence, along with valium, smoking, and excessive drinking; Miranda even spots Woody Allen, self-defined personification of urban neurosis, at the

[12] Paul Haspel, 'Ariel and Prospero's Modern-English Adventure: Language, Social Criticism, and Adaptation in Paul Mazursky's *Tempest*', *Literature/Film Quarterly* 34.2 (2006), pp. 130–139, pp. 130–1.

museum party. Phillip's only wish is to escape from all of this: he takes his daughter Miranda with him only as an afterthought, and the Ferdinand figure, Freddy, is an entirely unintended consequence of events rather than being any part of the Prospero-figure's plan. Here too Miranda and the Ariel figure, Aretha (Susan Sarandon), bond: Phillip asks 'What's with her?' and Aretha says 'It's called puberty'; she can talk much more easily to Miranda than her father can.

Mazursky's film has an openly psychologising approach: at an early stage, Phillip says 'I had the dream again, and the dog had it too'; later, Antonia says of the island: 'Very beautiful. Looks like a dream'. Aretha used to be married to a psychiatrist, and when Phillip says 'The problem is I found a white hair on my chest', Antonia answers 'The problem is you need help' – by which she clearly means therapy. In an apparent nod to the classic fodder of psychoanalysis, Phillip's father appears (to my knowledge the only appearance of the Prospero-figure's father in any version of *The Tempest*), and the fact that Phillip is 'consciously practising celibacy' certainly invites a psychologising reading.

Less openly stated, but arguably more subtly developed, are the ethnic tensions hinted at by the film. Miranda may say 'I'm an American', but on the island or in its vicinity the ingredients of the melting pot separate into their original identities as both Phillip and Alonso revert to type and reveal previously unsuspected fluency in Greek and Italian respectively. In so doing, they gesture delicately but unmistakably at the history of tension between Greeks and Italians in the Greek islands during the second world war – especially since Alonso's line of Italian is 'Siamo tutti pirati' ('We are all pirates') and he and his party are in one sense indeed invaders of Phillip's Greek retreat. This is an interesting analogue to the Spanish/Italian tensions explored in the original play, where the

Europeans are divided into two groups: the Milanese, represented by Prospero, Duke of Milan, his daughter Miranda and his brother Antonio; and the Neapolitans, comprising Alonso, King of Naples, his son Ferdinand, his brother Sebastian, and various of his counsellors. Shakespeare is very clear, and correct, about terming Milan a duchy and Naples a kingdom. Moreover, it is also notable that he draws a careful distinction in the nomenclature of the two groups: while Prospero and Antonio are clearly Italian in origin – Prospero shares a name with such historical figures as Prospero Adorno, Duke of Genoa, and Prospero Colonna, celebrated *condottiere* – the names of the Neapolitan characters are pointedly not so. Alonso and Ferdinand are both obviously Spanish, while Sebastian, the name of the last king of Portugal, had equally strong connections with the Iberian peninsula. To represent the rulers of Naples as being Spanish in origin is not another example of Shakespeare's celebrated geographical carelessness; unlike the notorious sea-coast of Bohemia in *The Winter's Tale*, it has a firm foundation in fact. Naples was part of the Kingdom of the Two Sicilies, which had for centuries been a bone of contention between would-be foreign conquerors. Coveted by the French, it had eventually fallen under the rule of Alfonso V of Aragon, after whose death it had broken loose from the Aragonese crown, which had passed to his brother John II, and had been seized by Alfonso's bastard son Ferrante. It had however still retained its strongly Aragonese feel, with its rulers being very clearly identifiable as Spanish. For all its apparent distance from the original text, Mazursky's *Tempest* can be seen as very close to it in this respect.

The 1992 *Animated Tales* version of *The Tempest*, which was, like all in this series, an improbable collaboration of Russian animators, Welsh producers and predominantly English actors, is also notable for its treatment of race and ethnicity. Although the showcasing of the harpies sequence serves as a real advert for what animation can do at points in the narrative where conventional adaptations might struggle, the technique has corresponding drawbacks. Being puppets, the characters struggle with emotion – not least because there is, as Laurie Osborne observes, a deliberate foregrounding of their physical puppetness[13] (though the film makes little use of the conceit that puppetness would so readily have allowed, which would have been to expose their existential puppetness too). Clear signals for emotion therefore have to be developed, and one of the ways in which this is done is through careful use of music. Very understated music over the opening narration is followed by storm sound effects. In general, music is used to supplement the language of appearance by acting like *leitmotiven* for certain characters and themes, most notably Ariel and the Miranda/Ferdinand romance (Caliban has none). It is also used to traditional filmic effect to heighten atmosphere and to point moments in the narrative. The music is generally modern in feel: at least some is synthesised, and there is an electric guitar at the end, in line with these productions' general brief to appeal to a contemporary audience.

The primary language used, however, is that of appearance. Blinking signifies sincerity and/or contentment, and characterisation is expressed principally by looks. Miranda (voiced by Katy Behean) is blonde and not unlike Cinderella in the Disney movie; lilies are visible behind her as she sleeps. Ariel is a little like an alien with wings. Ethereally pale, with a suggestion of the skeletal, and semi-transparent, with what looks like a tail, this Ariel is voiced by a

[13] Laurie E. Osborne, 'Poetry in Motion: Animating Shakespeare', in *Shakespeare the Movie: Popularizing the plays on film, tv, and video*, edited by Lynda E. Boose and Richard Burt (London: Routledge, 1997), pp. 103–120, p. 115.

woman, Ella Hood, and is defined almost entirely by appearance rather than action: Laurie Osborne comments that 'the one figure who exceeds the puppeteering powers of Prospero has her lines cut so that she is even more under his control than those he overtly stops and starts'.[14] Caliban (voiced by Alun Armstrong) has a Mohican haircut and a face that looks like a potato with a prognathous jaw, and is strongly reminiscent of Victorian anti-Irish caricatures of the O'Caliban. He has Vulcan-like ears and some kind of spines or ridges on his back, evoking an idea of the reptilian – perhaps specifically a dinosaur. Ferdinand, meanwhile, has a costume which colour-tones with Miranda's, indicating their coupledom, while both Antonio and Sebastian have substantial paunches.

Particularly important are noses (this is significant, given that Stanislav Sokolov's other contribution to the series, *The Winter's Tale*, does not distinguish characters by their noses). Antonio's bulbous nose makes him look Jewish, while Stephano has a sot's nose and Ariel's is childlike. Prospero (voiced by Timothy West) has a nose which is strong but unsinister, denoting his power and establishing him as a physical (and, by implication, moral) norm. He also has a blue cloak, the colour associated with holiness in the iconography of religious paintings, and resistance to him is significantly muted: when he says 'There's more work' and whispers to Ariel, Ariel says only 'My lord, it shall be done'. Equally there is no 'O my father, I have broke your hest to say so', and when Ferdinand and Miranda avow their love we cut straight to Prospero blinking approvingly; he then pronounces a blessing with no hint of disapproval, so that the impression created is that everything that happens is the product of Prospero's will. As we shall see, Jarman's film is virtually alone among close adaptations of *The Tempest* in being

14 Osborne, 'Poetry in Motion: Animating Shakespeare', p. 115.

able to entertain the idea of a Prospero whose authority is flawed and questionable.

In *The Animated Tales* version, there is certainly no sense of Caliban perhaps having a case, or of Prospero's conduct to him being in any way unjustified. Considering how much is necessarily cut for the 25-minute running time of this production, quite a bit of Stephano and Trinculo is retained, making this version seem much more comic than *The Tempest* often does, and Caliban's pleasure at attaining his 'Freedom' is undercut by the fact that he somersaults as he says it. The crucial line 'This thing of darkness I acknowledge mine' is spoken flatly and without emphasis (unsurprisingly, given Caliban's marked degree of difference from Prospero), and although we are told by a voice-over as the ship sails that Prospero 'Left behind that enchanted isle and its curious inhabitants', we have no real sense of who or what these might be, because we have seen only Caliban. The voice-over also says that 'His task fulfilled', 'Prospero, once again the rightful Duke of Milan, set sail to continue his fateful journey'; this evokes no specific location but acts as an emblem both of deferred closure and a metaphor of life, and clearly suggests that he is a figure guided by Providence. This is an idea further underlined by the fact that the production has a narrator (Martin Jarvis) – the device so beloved of 19th-century realist novels with providentialist overtones – who clearly controls how the characters are perceived: Prospero, for instance, is introduced as 'The poor, betrayed, and overthrown Duke of Milan'. Most notably, the accusation that 'The devil speaks in him' is rebutted by a stern 'No' from Prospero, which clearly invites us to infer that the opposite is in fact true.

The idea of the Christian which hovers around Prospero is accentuated by this version's marked downplaying of the classical elements of the play. The harpies – skeletal figures with grotesque breasts, presumably because the only thing to do with puppets is to exaggerate physical characteristics – are never named as such, and there is no masque, although a unicorn wanders on just after 'Our revels now are ended'. Ferdinand's Virgilian line 'Most sure, the goddess' is cut, leaving his first words as 'Oh, if a virgin', and so too is the accusation that the King has 'loosed (his daughter) to an African' – an omission which makes the play less open to accusations of racism but also removes the echoes of Virgil present in the original, where Claribel's new home of Tunis is explicitly identified as Dido's Carthage. The omission of the line 'Most sure, the goddess' also has other consequences: although one reference to possible goddesshood is retained, in Alonso's 'Is that the goddess that hath severed us?', Ferdinand's quick reply is 'Sir, she is mortal', and a Blakean-looking lightning cloud suggests divine intervention of an explicitly Christian rather than pagan kind. Moreover, the first line of Shakespeare spoken is 'Hell is empty, and all the devils are here', which, given the other suggestions of the numinous, takes on unusual theological force.

Ironically, considering the emphasis on ethnicity implied by the striking differences between noses, the actual setting of this adaptation is uncertain: we are told only that it is 'Somewhere between Tunis and Naples'. There is certainly little emphasis on any specific context; although the big overhearing statue – one of many heads in the landscape – is reminiscent of an Easter Island head, the unicorn, the fawn, and the ostrich, while they may be seen as economically and emblematically representing an element of the text, clearly relate most closely to a generic idea of the pastoral. (The unicorn, an animal which will proverbially come only to a virgin, is also reminiscent of the tiger in *Forbidden Planet*, which turns on Alta when she has kissed the Captain.) The effect created is of a decontextualised setting in which racial characteristics must be understood as innate and 'natural' rather than as the result of particular circumstances, while the resolutely Elizabethan costumes, like the Viking longship in Stow's version, silently deny any suggestion that the events could have any resonance outside Shakespeare's own time.

Even more interested in race, albeit with a very different emphasis, is a 1998 PG-rated made-for-TV version of the play set in the Mississippi bayous during the Civil War, and directed by Jack Bender. Bender's *The Tempest* is surprising in a number of ways. First, it alters the story of both the American Civil War and of *The Tempest*; there are some parallels here with a putative earlier version of *The Tempest* – Wellman's *Yellow Sky*. Also set in America, the opening caption of Wellman's version declares us to be in 'The West – 1867'; various characters are interrogated about which side they supported during the Civil War, and 'Grandpa' blames tthe war for the fact that 'Stretch' Dawson (Gregory Peck) has gone to the bad. As with *Forbidden Planet*, the dialogue of Bender's film intersects only minimally with the text of Shakespeare's *The Tempest*: not until the close do we hear a word of Shakespeare, when the hero, Gideon Prosper, throws his ring in the pond as a symbol of the renunciation of his power and says the 'Now my charms are all o'erthrown' lines from the Epilogue – the first (and only) lines from the play. Bender's *Tempest* is entirely transposed to an American setting: it is set first on a financially troubled plantation which is, in the opening scenes at least, reminiscent of *Gone With the Wind*, complete with a Southern belle named Sophie who is clearly a prospective second wife for Gideon. In fact, Sophie disappears from the narrative almost as soon as she has entered it, serving only to mark the difference (and the potential cause of a quarrel) between Gideon and his brother, Anthony. The only apparent link with the *Tempest* is that the ranch has 'Prosperity' written above it; over this we see 'Est. 1783', the year in which Britain recognised American independence. After the Prospero figure has been driven out from Prosperity, the setting then moves to an island in the bayou.

A number of other crucial elements of the play are also dislocated. Perhaps most notably, Azaleigh (Donzaleigh Abernathy) – the mambo priestess who teaches voodoo to 'Houngan' Gideon Prosper (Peter Fonda) – and, even more surprisingly, her son Ariel (Harold Perrineau), are both black. Traditional identities are complicated even further by the fact that Azaleigh is a good character, yet she is also structurally much more like Sycorax than any other character in *The Tempest*, since Ariel in the play has no mother. Conversely, Caliban is a poor white named Gatorman (though the German subtitles – the only version of the film currently available is marketed solely in Germany, under the title *Der Sturm* – call him 'Caliban');[15] he does, however, fulfil the central Caliban rôle when he says 'Before they came, this was my bayou'. The reasons for this reversal of the usual polarities are clear, even though not stated: it would be unthinkable to demonise African Americans in the way that is done to Caliban; instead, they must be treated with respect, not least because black soldiers have such a prominent presence in the US army, whose history is celebrated here. (That this Ariel is an African American is loudly spelled out for us, when he is asked where he comes from and says 'Africa. But I been working in Mississippi'.) Consequently Harold Perrineau, who had already played Mercutio in Baz Lurhmann's *William Shakespeare's Romeo + Juliet*, is given the substantial and presigious part of Ariel – in which he is allowed to do far more, and display far greater independence and influence, than is usual – and black culture is validated in

[15] It is also intriguing that in German, Ariel addresses Prosper by the formal 'Sie'.

Azaleigh and her Mambo magic. One of the incidental consequences of this is that Prospero cannot drown his books because
there are none – here, magic is strictly an oral tradition, as voodoo
was for African American slaves. The extent of the reversal of the
customary polarities is neatly indicated when Anthony hunts Ariel
and shoots him – a structural inversion of what is done to Caliban in
the Stow film, which reveals the enormous ideological shifts that
have occurred in conceptions of race between 1908 and 1998,
and between Edwardian England and late 20th-century America.

There are, however, two remaining taboos which Bender's film is
not prepared to tackle. Firstly, Caliban is not, as might perhaps
have been expected, a Native American; instead John Pyper-
Ferguson, who plays Caliban, is actually Australian, removing the
problem of Caliban from the American sphere altogether (nor is
there any indication that anyone other than white masters and
black slaves may ever have lived in the US). Secondly, there is no
Claribel figure, so no marriage to an 'African'; in addition the friend-
ship between Miranda and Ariel, though close, is painstakingly
established as platonic. Miscegenation, it seems, is still the love that
dare not speak its name, and perhaps this is one of the reasons why
Caliban is white, since to make him so means avoiding not only the
question of Native Americans but also even the faintest suggestion
of sexual relations across the race divide. (Similarly, there is no
mention of who Ariel's father was, but the darkness of his skin leaves
no doubt that he must have been black.)

The idea of mixed-race relationships would of course have been
particularly abhorrent in the 19th-century South, and that setting
pervades every element of the narrative. The Ferdinand character,
Captain Frederick Allen (who seems to owe something to Leslie
Nielsen's Captain Adams in *Forbidden Planet*), is an old-fashioned
southern gentleman, and we are forcibly reminded of the ideologi-

cal implications of the American Civil War when Anthony (the Antonio character, played by John Glover) says to his brother, 'Gideon, you're sounding more like one of those Yankee abolition-ists every day' – while Ariel, who doesn't want freedom, just to get to General Grant's headquarters to help him, wants to go to fight for the Union because of Lincoln's Emancipation Proclamation. It is here, rather than in any story of forgiveness or love, that we find the emotional heart and teleological energies of the narrative. Initially, when Ariel mentions General Grant's headquarters, Gideon says 'I've told you, there's nothing there to interest us'. Later he repeats that he does not care about the war, but Ariel demands, 'How you don't care? That's like saying you don't care if your house is burning down'. At this point, the narrative voiceover from Gideon declares that 'I did not see it then, but the truth of Ariel's words was about to shatter our world', and indeed Gideon's house nearly *does* catch fire when he lets a magical flame land on the floor. Gideon repeatedly resists involvement in the war; even when Ariel shames him by asking him if he plans to 'whup' him like his brother did, he goes no further than giving Ariel permission to help General Grant if he wishes. Although Miranda, in the adaptation's only glance at the classical, compares the war to that between the Greeks and the Trojans, bestowing on it the importance and resonance of legend (appropriately enough given the Christian name of General Ulysses Grant), Gideon still will not intervene until he asks Ariel 'My brother says I'm isolated and selfish ... Is that true?', and Ariel replies, 'Yes, sir'. Even though commitment to the war is clearly represented as a good thing, it is also apparent that this fighting has its price: when in Prosper's service Ariel can become a bird; out of it he is free but can no longer fly.

Prosper's final decision that he *does* care, and that he will intervene to help General Grant, provides the emotional climax of the film. He comes to help disguised as an American eagle, in one of the many human-to-bird transformations in the film; these may perhaps owe something to Ursula LeGuin's similarly race-bending narrative *A Wizard of Earthsea*, where it is not revealed until the second book, *The Tombs of Atuan*, that the hero Ged, who transforms into a sparrowhawk, is dark-skinned and that the Kargish 'barbarians' are light-skinned. It is also Gideon who provides the film's clarification of its own theme when he says 'North and South. Brother killing brother'. Though it proves impossible for the two sides to be immediately reconciled – Gideon offers his hand but Anthony says 'You're a fool' and is taken away to be tried by a military court – forgiveness and reconciliation are stressed elsewhere when Ariel intercedes for Gatorman on the grounds that he will be useful in helping them to pack, and when Prosper calls Miranda and Frederick's marriage a 'union'. Clearly Bender is attracted to the play because the brother metaphor maps so neatly onto his view of the Civil War – the South is in the wrong but Gideon recuperates it – and because Miranda's marriage to Ferdinand offers so convenient a metaphor for bridging the gap.

This schematic approach does not, however, preclude a crafted attention to other concerns in the film. There is, for instance, frantic intercutting between Anthony at the ball, Ariel being whipped, and Gideon learning magic: Anthony is revealed to be callous, but Gideon, like Prospero, is careless not to know what is happening to the slaves on his plantation. This stress on the craft of the narrative is important, because the film is very committed to the importance and value of difficulty: magic is difficult to learn, and easy to lose – Ariel now regrets not having learned voodoo from his mother, and Gideon, unlike his original in the play, involuntarily loses the ability to do magic at one point when his faith falters. Not only does Gideon still have 'much to learn' about magic; he is also clearly stupid about Miranda, as Ariel plainly tells him: 'Guess you some kind of Jehovah, gonna forbid her to eat the fruit of the tree of know-ledge'. Unlike his counterpart in the play, Gideon takes no visible interest in Miranda's education, and it is not until scene vii (37 minutes into the film) that he tells Miranda about her past. (Perhaps unsurprisingly, she doesn't take it well, because she is horrified that he has lied about it.) Nor has Gideon engineered a marriage for her; indeed, like Phillip in Mazursky's *Tempest*, he has no prior knowledge of the Ferdinand character and definitely wants revenge, and when Ferdinand wants to get back to his regiment, saying that it is a holy war, Gideon – who is not testing him but genuinely trying to get rid of him – is minded to help him on his way.

In keeping with Gideon's general lack of concern about Miranda's developing sexuality, this adaptation has minimal interest in the psychoanalytic or even the psychological. So far from Miranda being kept in ignorance of Ariel's existence, she and Ariel are seen *tête-à-tête*; there can, therefore, be no suggestion that Ariel is in any sense an emanation of Prosper's mind. Moreover, Gideon's concern that the Ferdinand figure should be honourable seems much more reasonable here, in the context of a war and when 'Ferdinand' is a stranger whom he does not know at all and whom he did not lure to join them. (In deference to American values of merit rather than birth, there is never any suggestion that the Ferdinand character's parentage is in any way special or significant.) The nearest we come to any sense that what happens inside the mind may be more important than reality is during the scene in which Gideon seems to recover his magic and to disguise himself as Miranda bathing and then sees Anthony, which later seems not really to have happened. Anthony thinks it was all a dream, and maybe it was, since Gideon subsequently says that he still hasn't got his magic back. The only other hint at the psychological is when Anthony and the Gonzalo figure are caught between Gatorman and the disguised Ariel: as if the plot of *The Tempest* is going wrong, there is a brief psychomachia before they choose Gatorman as their guide. This is, however, entirely logical, since Gatorman names Prosper and offers them the solid inducement of being able to track him down.

The workings of the mind are downplayed in Bender's film because what really matters here are the workings of God. Above all else, this adaptation is pious, and the Christian God proves surprisingly able to coexist quite happily with Baron Samedi and the other supernatural figures on whom Gideon calls. (Again, there is a parallel here with *Yellow Sky*, where 'Stretch' Dawson swears on the Bible and eventually returns the money.) Ferdinand asks Miranda not whether she is a goddess, but 'Are you an angel?' – a question which not only abolishes the classical connotations of Shakespeare's *Tempest* but also vigorously asserts a Christian one. Later, he buries an enemy soldier, puts a cross on the grave and saying 'In the name of the father, the son and the holy ghost', crossing himself. Perhaps the ranch should have been called 'Providence' rather than 'Prosperity', for that, ultimately, is the keynote of this film.

Many directors, then, have found *The Tempest* to be a play which speaks eloquently to a wide range of concerns. Few, though, have taken as many risks with it as Fred Wilcox, director of the first of this book's three 'case study' adaptations, *Forbidden Planet*.

forbidden planet
(dir. Fred Wilcox, 1956)

The central question in relation to *Forbidden Planet* is a very simple one: is it or isn't it an adaptation of *The Tempest*? There is certainly no mention of Shakespeare anywhere in the film credits, and there are some significant differences of plot and emphasis. No one dies during the course of *The Tempest*, but several crewmen and, most importantly, Dr Morbius are casualties in *Forbidden Planet*. As Anthony Miller points out, 'unlike Prospero returning to his dukedom, Morbius does not return to earth';[1] instead, Robby does, inverting the logic of the original ending entirely. John Jolly further declares that 'As for Caliban and the Id monster, they are alike only inasmuch as both are creatures of darkness; otherwise the two characters are genres apart'.[2] Most notably, events are seen through the eyes of the incomers rather than the residents, completely inverting the experience of watching *The Tempest*, where we are properly introduced first to the inhabitants of the island and only belatedly to the newcomers. As the captain announces at the beginning of *Forbidden Planet*, 'Stand by to reverse polarity'.

[1] Anthony Miller, '"In this last tempest": Modernising Shakespeare's *Tempest* on Film', *Sydney Studies in English* 23 (1997), pp. 24–40.

[2] John Jolly, 'The Bellerophon Myth and *Forbidden Planet*', *Extrapolation* 27.1 (1986), pp. 84–90, p. 85.

The most sustained attack on the general association between *Forbidden Planet* and *The Tempest* has come from Judith Buchanan, who points out that the film

> ... was not advertised with any claim of a Shakespearean associ-
> ation during its early exhibition runs or in its press releases. As a
> landmark production for MGM, and a costly one, it was much
> reviewed in the year of its release ... Not one of these contem-
> porary reviews mentions a Shakespearean resonance to the film.

Buchanan observes that 'The earliest published comment con-
necting *Forbidden Planet* to *The Tempest* that I have been able to
trace was made by Kingsley Amis in 1961', and though 'in 1975,
Irving Block, who had co-written the story upon which the screenplay was based, emerged from the shadows to tell *Cinéfantastique*
that it had been he who had "suggested they use Shakespeare's
The Tempest as a premise on which to build the science fiction
story"', Buchanan is sceptical about this, suggesting instead that the
two texts may share a Jungian archetype. (She also points to the
strong parallels with *The Tempest* in the 1932 horror film *The Island of
Lost Souls*, an adaptation of *The Island of Dr Moreau*, which no one
had ever previously considered as alluding to *The Tempest*;[3] in a
later work she adds to this the suggestion that *Iguana* (dir. Monte
Hellman, 1988) is also a version of *The Tempest*. In both cases,
however, she sees them less as adaptations than as analogues.)[4]

[3] Judith Buchanan, '*Forbidden Planet* and the Retrospective Attribution of
Intentions', in *Retrovisions: Reinventing the Past in Film and Fiction*, edited by
Deborah Cartmell, I. Q. Hunter, and Imelda Whelehan (London: Pluto, 2001), pp.
148–162, pp. 149, 150, 152–3, and 154–5.

[4] Judith Buchanan, *Shakespeare on Film* (Longman: Pearson, 2005), p. 90.

Other critics have generally been more willing to accept the link. Ace Pilkington calls *Forbidden Planet* an 'obvious re-writing',[5] and Alden T. Vaughan and Virginia Mason Vaughan in their magisterial *Shakespeare's Caliban: A Cultural History* simply state that

> The most successful screen version of *The Tempest*, at least in terms of popular appeal and longevity, is the science-fiction film *Forbidden Planet*. Although it abandons Shakespeare's language entirely, its central conflict between the conveniences of technology and the terror of science's destructive power captures the serious elements of Prospero's magic in ways the television presentations of the British Broadcasting Corporation (BBC) and the Bard do not.[6]

Similarly, Merrell Knighten speaks of 'the wholesale and unblushing reproduction of situation, story, character, and characterization' from *The Tempest* in *Forbidden Planet*,[7] while Tim Youngs writes, 'John Brosnan reports that *The Tempest* "happened to be special effects man Irving Block's favourite play, and it was Block, along with writing collaborator Allen Adler, who wrote the story for the movie"'.[8]

[5] Ace Pilkington, 'Zeffirelli's Shakespeare', in *Shakespeare and the Moving Image: The Plays on Film and Television*, edited by Anthony Davies and Stanley Wells (Cambridge: Cambridge University Press, 1994), pp. 163–179, p. 164.

[6] Alden T. Vaughan and Virginia Mason Vaughan, *Shakespeare's Caliban: A Cultural History* (Cambridge: Cambridge University Press, 1991), p. 200.

[7] Merrell Knighten, 'The Triple Paternity of *Forbidden Planet*', *Shakespeare Bulletin* 12.3 (summer, 1994), pp. 36–37, p. 36.

[8] Tim Youngs, 'Cruising against the Id: The Transformation of Caliban in *Forbidden Planet*', in *Constellation Caliban: Figurations of a Character*, edited by Nadia Lie and Theo D'haen (Amsterdam: Rodopi, 1997), pp. 211–229, p. 213, n. 2.

There are numerous similarities between *Forbidden Planet* and *The Tempest*. *Forbidden Planet*'s reference to the 'Conquest and colonisation of deep space' announces the central theme of *The Tempest*, and the Trinculo figure's dismissal of 'Another one of them new worlds – no beer, no women, no pool parlors, nothing' is surely as unmistakable as it is ironic. The question which a crew member asks of Robby, 'Is it a male or a female?', directly echoes the Victorian tradition of casting a woman as Ariel and the habitual gender uncertainty associated with spirits, as explained by Milton in *Paradise Lost*. Anthony Miller points out that 'Renaissance magic is translated into breathtakingly advanced technologies' and that 'The Gonzalo of *Forbidden Planet* steps from his spaceship and rhapsodises prosaically on the planet Altair: "Look at the colour of that sky ... a man could learn to live here and to love it"';[9] as J. P. Telotte observes, 'While one speaker views the planet Altair IV as wondrous and awe-inspiring, the other reads it more skeptically, as just another planet, lacking some very basic human satisfactions',[10] just as the Neapolitan courtiers disagree about what they see on the island. As Robert F. Willson points out, Alta 'has had a nightmare about an attack on the visitors' ship and is concerned about the safety of the crew; her lines call up those of Miranda from I.ii, where she witnesses the apparent wrecking of Alonso's ship in a storm: "O, I have suffered/With those I saw suffer!"'.[11] There are two sculptures of fish in Morbius's house, incongruous on this planet where water features only as a swimming pool, yet perfectly logical in the island

[9] Miller, '"In this last tempest"', *Sydney Studies in English* 23 (1997), p. 25.

[10] J. P. Telotte, 'Science Fiction in Double Focus: *Forbidden Planet*', *Film Criticism* 13.3 (1989), pp. 25–36, p. 26.

[11] Robert F. Willson, Jr, *Shakespeare in Hollywood, 1929–1956* (London: Associated University Presses, 2000), p. 105.

setting of *The Tempest*; indeed, as Sara Martin notes, 'Morbius epitomises the idea that every man is an island'.[12] When Morbius plays Krell[13] music, we may recall 'The isle is full of noises' (although Alden T. Vaughan and Virginia Mason Vaughan see this as 'his particular masque'),[14] and when Adams has to be reminded to discipline the cook, we surely hear echoes of 'I had forgot that foul conspiracy/Of the beast Caliban and his confederates' (IV.i.139–40) – especially since the cook neatly collapses in himself the rôles of Stephano and Trinculo.

The central concerns of *The Tempest* are also echoed in *Forbidden Planet*. Morbius has a cave leading out of his study; Prospero lives in a cave. The Utopia discussion of *The Tempest* is reprised when Morbius tells us: 'In times long past, this planet was the home of a mighty and noble race of beings' – better and stronger than humans. (Indeed, Ruth Morse characterises the history of the relationship between *The Tempest* and science fiction as 'political, and involv(ing) questions of power and the responsi-bility of the scientist, of the definition of civilization and the "were-I-human"'.)[15] Though 'This all but divine race perished', with the loss of 'Their cloud-piercing towers', their technology still survives (there is a small irony here in that *Forbidden Planet* itself is at the time of writing available only on video, a technology which will

[12] Sara Martin, 'Classic Shakespeare for All: *Forbidden Planet* and *Prospero's Books*, Two Screen Adaptations of *The Tempest*', in *Classics in Film and Fiction*, edited by Deborah Cartmell, I. Q. Hunter, Heidi Kaye and Imelda Whelehan (London: Pluto, 2000), pp. 34–53, p. 41.

[13] The word is spelt variously Krel or Krell by different critics; since there seems to be no standard version, I have felt at liberty to adopt the one I prefer.

[14] Vaughan and Vaughan, *Shakespeare's Caliban*, p. 205.

[15] Ruth Morse, 'Monsters, Magicians, Movies: *The Tempest* and the Final Frontier', *Shakespeare Survey* 53 (2000), pp. 164–174, p. 164.

surely soon be obsolete). Finally, Morbius's remark to Alta that 'These gentlemen have expressed a very kindly concern over the amount of liberty you have here' closely echoes *The Tempest*'s concern with the idea of freedom (the last word of the play is 'free'), and even Buchanan herself concedes that 'The action of *Forbidden Planet*, like that of *The Tempest* in 1611, is located at the remote borders of what can be conceived in its contemporary world',[16] though here the frontier has become the perimeter, and it is as important, or more so, to keep things out as to expand one's territory.

Forbidden Planet and *The Tempest* even share what might be termed the same paratexts, since when Morbius tells us that 'Some dark, terrible, incomprehensible force' was responsible for the deaths of all of his companions by tearing them limb from limb, we may well remember either or both of *Dr Faustus* and *Frankenstein* – the second owing a considerable debt to *The Tempest* and the first a probable source for it: both Faustus and Prospero have been related to the figure of Dr John Dee, and the name of each can be roughly translated as 'lucky', so that Celia Daileader simply calls *The Tempest* 'Shakespeare's answer to *Faustus*'.[17] The historical events on which *The Tempest* draws seem also to be remembered: Morbius doesn't want help any more than those shipwrecked on Bermuda did, and Alta/Altaira is called after Altair 4, just as Bermuda Rolfe and Virginia Dare – the first white children to be born in Bermuda and North America respectively – were named after the strange new lands in which they were born. Moreover, the fawn and tiger cohabit, as in the Garden of Eden, which provided the

---

[16] Buchanan, *Shakespeare on Film*, p. 152.

[17] Celia R. Daileader, *Eroticism on the Renaissance Stage: Transcendence, Desire, and the Limits of the Visible* (Cambridge: Cambridge University Press, 1998), p.17.

foundational concept for the pastoral discourse on which *The Tempest* draws so freely. Also redolent of Eden is the fact that Alta is clearly naked when swimming – she even asks 'What's a bathing suit?' – although, in an obvious continuity glitch presumably forced on the director for reasons of modesty, she is decorously clothed when she emerges. *Forbidden Planet*'s use of classical material and its reference to 'cloud-piercing towers of glass and porcelain and adamantine steel' echo not only *The Tempest*'s 'cloud-capped towers' (IV.i.152) but also H. G. Wells's *The Time Machine*, a novel which makes much use of *Tempest* motifs, while there is a clear parallel between the lost city of the Krell and the lost city of Kôr in Rider Haggard's *She*, a text with a number of Shakespearean allusions, not least to *The Tempest*. Finally, there seem to be one or two small gestures towards an earlier putative version of *The Tempest*, Wellman's *Yellow Sky*. The space crew land in the desert as the outlaws are driven into it in *Yellow Sky*; they say 'Look at the colour of that sky'; and Farman's sarcastic comment ('Rank does have its little privileges') when the Captain prevents him from seeing Alta recalls the way in which 'Stretch' Dawson in *Yellow Sky* similarly uses his authority over the men to requisition the only girl. In both films, too, that one girl is represented as an instinctive tease.

Although *Forbidden Planet* does indeed relate very closely to *The Tempest*, there is not a simple one-on-one correspondence. Most notably, it is not always clear who is equivalent to whom: there is competition in particular for the rôles of Ferdinand and Prospero. Ostensibly, it seems clear that Morbius, the existing inhabitant of the planet and father of the Miranda figure, is Prospero, and that the younger, incoming Captain Adams is Ferdinand; indeed there is a moment where Morbius 'invites' Captain Adams to disarm just as Prospero forcibly deprives Ferdinand of his weapon. However,

Adams is neither as young nor anything like as helpless as Ferdinand is, and rather than playing out any plan of Morbius's as Ferdinand does of Prospero's, Adams makes his own destiny. Aspects of Prospero's rôle in *The Tempest* accrue to Adams rather than to Morbius; Robert F. Willson observes, 'The function of Prospero as protector of his daughter's virginity is ... transferred to Adams', and 'While Ariel was the character who offered insights about compassion and forgiveness to Prospero, Adams as hero is given the task of pronouncing *Planet*'s moral to the keeper of the Krell secrets'. The difference between the two is further collapsed in that '... to Adams, the cook's behavior is just one more sign of the planet's corrupting influence on his crew. Both Adams and Dr Morbius share a concern about the effect of such influences on their "missions"'. There are also parallels between Morbius and Caliban which are apparent even before the film's final revelation: 'That the monster is the id further suggests that Morbius's desire to keep his daughter captive can be understood as latently incestuous. Here we can see parallels between the father's desire and that of Caliban'.[18]

In a similar confusion of rôles, Robby has elements of both Caliban and Ariel: 'Robby combines the character traits of Ariel and Caliban: he implements the "magic" of his inventor Dr Morbius, but he also takes care of the household chores'.[19] He is helpful to the humans, as is Ariel, but his participation in the structural equivalent of the Trinculo scene aligns him with the Caliban rôle, especially since for a large part of the film it is not obvious where that is to be located otherwise. Alden T Vaughan and Virginia Mason Vaughan ask,

[18] Willson, *Shakespeare in Hollywood, 1929–1956*, pp. 103–4 and 106.
[19] Willson, *Shakespeare in Hollywood, 1929–1956*, p. 102.

Where does Caliban fit into this sci-fi drama? In one sense, he is not a character in the film; in another sense, he is ever-present, though visible only through special effects. His shape, a Grendel-like monster, is revealed by electromagnetic currents as he crosses the spaceship's electrical fence and tears several spacemen apart (again, in Grendel fashion).

For them, Caliban is 'Dr Morbius's (Walter Pidgeon's) destructive impulse, ready to kill rather than be suppressed',[20] and this certainly does seem to be the case – not least when Robby says 'Nothing coming this way' just before the fence registers the presence of the id, failing to warn the crew in a way explicable only by assuming that he cannot betray the presence of the id because to do so would be to betray his master. The association of the monster with Morbius is also supported by Simone Caroti's suggestion that '"Morbius" is a slight reconfiguration of the Latin *morbus* and the Italian *morbo*, both names meaning "disease"'[21] and by the alternative etymology proposed by Seth Lerer: 'Dressed in black, with that Mephistophelean goatee and widow's peak, he is the very icon of death that is the etymon of his name'.[22] (This is not, however, the only derivation proposed for Morbius's name: Anthony Miller says that it 'combines words for death (*mors*) and life (*bios*) as well as carrying overtones of disease (*morbus*)';[23] John Jolly declares that '"Edward" signifies "prosperous guardian" and

---

[20] Vaughan and Vaughan, *Shakespeare's Caliban*, pp. 205 and 3.

[21] Simone Caroti, 'Science Fiction, *Forbidden Planet*, and Shakespeare's *The Tempest*', *Comparative Literature and Culture* 6.1 (March, 2004). Online: http://clcwebjournal.lib.purdue.edu/clcweb04-1/caroti04.html

[22] Seth Lerer, '*Forbidden Planet* and the Terrors of Philology', *Raritan* 19.3 (Winter 2000), pp. 73–86, p. 80.

[23] Miller, '"In this last tempest"', p. 33.

"Morbius" suggests "sickness"';[24] and J. P. Telotte suggests that 'Morbius' name seems to combine the Latin *morbidus* and *morbus*, words that denote "disease" and ultimately "death." At the same time, it recalls the Mobius strip, which turns upon itself to create a visual effect whereby its outside edge is also its inside'.[25] One might also wonder whether the name recalls Moby Dick, with the intangible id-monster as the white whale.) However, the Vaughans' mention of Grendel is suggestive, because the id-monster clearly does have antecedents quite different from those of Shakespeare's Caliban – not least the theories of Freud, of which Shakespeare of course had no knowledge. Caliban may be replaced here by the id-monster, but the id-monster is not 'simply' Caliban.

A less ambiguous link between *Forbidden Planet* and *The Tempest* is that the classical theme in *Forbidden Planet*, though understated, is very important. John Jolly points out that 'Block's predilection for myths open to mechanistic interpretations manifests itself not only in *Forbidden Planet*, but also in his 1957 film *Kronos*',[26] and in *Forbidden Planet*, though the emphasis is all nominally on the future, the past nevertheless remains central. The entire plot is predicated on the fact that a spaceship called the *Bellerophon* landed on Altair IV 20 years ago; the present crew are looking for survivors. The name Bellerophon is a resonant one. In Greek myth, Bellerophon was the grandson of Sisyphus, the king who was punished in Hades by having to forever roll up a hill a stone which forever rolled back down again. Bellerophon travelled to Tiryns, where Stheneboea, the wife of Proteus, king of Tiryns, falsely claimed that he had tried to seduce her. Because Proteus

[24] Jolly, 'The Bellerophon Myth and *Forbidden Planet*', p. 90, n. 7.

[25] Telotte, 'Science Fiction in Double Focus: *Forbidden Planet*', p. 36, n. 5.

[26] Jolly, 'The Bellerophon Myth and *Forbidden Planet*', p. 86.

was unwilling to harm Bellerophon openly, he sent him to Stheneboea's father Iobates, who set Bellerophon a series of tasks in the hope that he would die performing them. Amongst these was fighting the Chimaera, which Bellerophon accomplished on Pegasus, a horse spawned from the drops of blood dropped from the Gorgon's head, by flying over the monster and stuffing its jaws with lead: when it breathed fire, the lead melted and choked it. Bellerophon also defeated the Amazons, the fierce warrior women, but at the end of his life his two children were slain by the gods and he himself tried to fly on Pegasus to Olympus to remonstrate with the gods, but was flung down by Zeus. Crippled by the fall, he wandered the earth as an outcast.[27] The relevance of this story to *Forbidden Planet* is pointedly underlined in the film by Morbius's remark, 'Be sure and look only in the mirror. One does not behold the face of the Gorgon and live', reminding us that Bellerophon's horse, who ultimately betrayed him, was spawned from the Gorgon's blood. Equally, as John Jolly sums up, Morbius 'resembles the Greek hero Bellerophon insofar as he unwittingly carries his own death warrant to Altair IV and falls victim to hubris after gaining access to the Krell machine'.[28] Bellerophon's story also has other resonances: both the Chimaera and the flying horse raise the same kinds of questions about the borderline between the human and the nonhuman as Robby the Robot and the id-monster do, while the unhappy close of Bellerophon's life may perhaps trouble the apparent optimism of the film's ending.

The relevance of apparently arcane information such as the Bellerophon myth to the interpretation of *Forbidden Planet* is further underlined by the fact that Morbius is a philologist (one of the film's

[27] *New Larousse Encyclopedia of Mythology* (London: Hamlyn, 1959), pp. 182–3.
[28] Jolly, 'The Bellerophon Myth and *Forbidden Planet*', p. 84.

more hilarious moments is when someone explains to him what a philologist is), and it is his knowledge of languages which has given him access to Krell science. In an ingenious article, Seth Lerer points out that 'science fiction and philology have long shared an uneasy alliance. In Orwell's *1984*, the ill-fortuned Syme appears as the philological specialist in Newspeak'. Lerer argues that

> Morbius embodies ... a distinctively American response to the incursions of an émigré literary study into the academy and popular culture of the 1950s. His visage, his bearing, his pursuits, and his demise all cluster around a set of social and historical events that were reshaping literary and linguistic study in the postwar period.

For Lerer, Morbius's profession is not incidental but crucial, and points squarely at the wave of scholarly flight from Nazi persecutions in the late 1930s:

> 'Exile or collaborator?, asked the American academy of him and his ilk ... When Morbius at the movie's end recognizes his own responsibility for the monster that destroyed his shipmates and threatens to destroy his daughter ... he voices a larger concern about the guilt of those who made it out.

This context is underlined by the fact that, as Lerer notes, 'Morbius consistently uses the word "race" to describe (the Krell)', as well as by the timescale insisted on in the film:

> Twenty years before, Morbius stood by as his crew was murdered, only he and his wife saved. Twenty years before – that is, twenty years before 1956 – came the first waves of exile. In

•

1936, Auerbach was dismissed from Marburg and went to Istanbul; Curtius arrived at Hopkins; Jaeger showed up at Harvard ... Morbius explicitly refers to the destruction of his crew ... as 'the holocaust'.[29]

Lerer's points about race and displacement should certainly alert us to an important concern of the film. Tim Youngs comments pithily that 'Adams's spaceship is a *United Planets* cruiser. It is united by its crew's colour and gender'.[30] However, though the crew is indeed entirely male and white (notably unlike the crew of the USS *Enterprise* not very long afterwards), significant differences of origin are nevertheless hinted at by their names, which include the doctor Ostrow (Polish?), Dirocco (Italian), Lindstrom (Swedish) and Moran and Quin (Irish), as well as the hero Adams and his sidekick, the neatly named (for an astronaut) Farman, whom the captain introduces as 'my executive'. In the context of philology, it is particularly clear that we need to pay attention to this naming pattern. In the cultural imaginary of *Forbidden Planet*, it seems that the interracial tensions which have so often been seen as emblematised in the figure of Caliban have vanished without trace in the American melting pot, but in fact a hierarchy is still clearly apparent, and the WASP Captain is at the top of it as much as Captain Kirk will be above his interracial crew in Gene Roddenberry's *Star Trek*.

The stress on origins of languages in *Forbidden Planet*, then, clearly figures the classical past which is so important in *The Tempest*; it also evokes some interesting faultlines. Morbius's status as a philologist enacts a blurring between literature and science

[29] Lerer, '*Forbidden Planet* and the Terrors of Philology', pp. 74, 75, and 84.
[30] Youngs, 'Cruising against the Id', p. 228.

which parallels both the confused status of *Forbidden Planet* as a version of *The Tempest* and of science fiction itself as a literary genre. As Sara Martin notes, though received as a children's film – partly because its director made his reputation with *Lassie Come Home* (1943) – '*Forbidden Planet* was conceived as a high-budget film aiming at making science fiction respectable'.[31] Little has been made of the link between *Forbidden Planet* and *Lassie Come Home*, beyond Tim Youngs's tongue-in-cheek remark that 'The question of why the director of *Lassie Come Home* should have turned to a science-fiction version of the "puppy-headed monster," as Caliban is called by Trinculo (II.ii.154–55), is not one I shall doggedly pursue'.[32] In a way, though, the biological essentialism implicit in *Lassie Come Home*, which is predicated on differences in behaviour and nature between dogs and humans, is central to *Forbidden Planet*, because the latter opposes two areas of expertise – mind and body – as seen in the chiasmus of the exchange between Ostrow and Morbius: 'Doctor, how did you come by such a mechanism?' 'Er, I didn't come by him, doctor'. The men have the same title, and yet operate in diametrically opposed spheres and ways, with radically different areas of expertise. There is, however, no question about which of them is better equipped to advise and diagnose: when Morbius, looking at the nubile Alta, says 'I suppose one day I shall be obliged to make the trip to earth for the sake of her natural development', the more observant Ostrow quickly replies, 'I should say fairly soon too'. Moreover, Alta herself is a product of a fusion of mind and body, since while Morbius himself represents the intellectual, almost his only reference to his wife identifies her roundly with the physical:

[31] Martin, 'Classic Shakespeare for All', p. 39.

[32] Youngs, 'Cruising against the Id', p. 211.

'Look under biochemistry – Julia Morrison'. It is presumably also this safely WASP-sounding maternal ancestry, and the resulting blonde hair, which redeems Alta from the taint of her 'foreign' father, giving something of the flavour of a Shlyock/Jessica element to their relationship as well as a Prospero/Miranda one.

Indeed, texts and influences other than *The Tempest* are certainly important to *Forbidden Planet*, and they are by no means all Shakespearean. When Alta says 'I've always so terribly wanted to meet a young man, and now three of them at once', she is unnervingly reminiscent of Lucy in *Dracula*, who receives three proposals in one day and wishes she could accept them all. After the doctor disobeys the order that the Captain will have first go at the IQ booster, he emerges with a mark on his forehead, just like Mina in *Dracula*. The discourse of evolution, which is prominent in *Dracula*, is also important in *Forbidden Planet*: Morbius says 'The beast – the mindless primitive – even the Krell must have evolved from that beginning', and the doctor declares of the claw, 'This thing runs counter to every known law of adaptive evolution', adding 'Anywhere in the galaxy, this thing is a nightmare'. However, there is a definite tension between this and the much more overtly religious perspective implied by lines such as the Captain's 'the secret devil of every soul on the planet', and the fact that Morbius and his wife (whom he married on board ship) survived alone on the planet, making them Adam and Eve figures. This tension is neatly emblematised in the fact that the Skipper's question, 'How do these continents check with the old charts?', with its implicit suggestion of flux and change, comes immediately after the declaration that 'The Lord sure makes some beautiful worlds'; while Ostrow says of Alta, 'The view looks just like heaven', and the cook, with delicious irony, tells Robby the Robot, 'You're the most understanding soul I ever met up with'. Religion appears to win the battle of the two discourses: although part of the initial publicity read 'See the thrilling romance of an Earthman and a captive planet goddess!',[33] with a surprising suggestion of polytheism, there are clearly Christian overtones in lines such as 'The lord sure makes some beautiful worlds'. Moreover, the three principal spacemen, Ostrow, Farman, and Adams, are like a parodic Trinity, with one ultimately sacrificing himself to save the rest of the crew. Most notably, the last word in the film is 'God'. Nevertheless, one of the most haunting images in the film is that of crosses in the alien planetscape, and there is a question mark over Robby's status as a 'creation' and what this may say about 'creator(s)' – especially since Ostrow thinks what the Krell did was 'true creation'. After all, the credits read 'Introducing Robby, the Robot', as if Robby were a real person – as if, in short, robotics were a real possibility and human intellect not the ultimate *telos* of development.

Nor does *Forbidden Planet* offer the same kinds of suggestion about setting as The *Tempest*. Whereas *The Tempest* gestures towards a world in which America is still an unexplored, undefined dream, *Forbidden Planet*, for all its nominal setting on Altair IV, supplies a concretely and specifically American framework: consider for instance its reference to 'the head of the arroyo' and the cook's wish for 'Genuine Kansas City Bourbon' (the latter also bringing with it a faint whiff of *The Wizard of Oz*). As Seth Lerer points out,

> ... what Morbius has recreated on his stage set of discovery is
> nothing less than the American dream: a Southern California-

[33] Quoted in Buchanan, '*Forbidden Planet* and the Retrospective Attribution of Intentions', p. 159.

style high modernist household, complete with landscape, furnishings, and elevations right out of, say, the work of Marcel Breuer, Mies van der Rohe, or Richard Neutra ... designed out of the building blocks of émigré modernism.[34]

Forbidden Planet certainly taps into some distinctively American concerns of the period. As Judith Buchanan remarks, reading it in relation to McCarthyism and its fear of the enemy within, 'Despite its psychoanalytic terminology and central interest in Morbius's inner turmoil, the film's concern with the theme of inner conflict extends to a societal as well as to a psychological level'.[35] This is eerily emblematised in the idea of the shared dream, when Alta while asleep appears to have had access to her father's thoughts and to have divined Adams's danger. Not much later, shared, state-programmed dreaming was to be a characteristic of the tyrannical dystopia which America had become in Philip K. Dick's 1960s classic, *Galactic Pot-healer*; in both cases it clearly offers an ironic commentary on the 'American dream'. Equally, Anthony Miller argues that 'The overmastering scientific organisation of the Krell, their faith that the limitations of human nature may be overcome by material means, must in some degree allude to the Marxist experiment and its ideal of the scientific perfectibility of society',[36] and hence to the fear of Communism which so traumatised 1950s America.

Forbidden Planet is certainly a film which worries about who owns what. As Tim Youngs remarks,

[34] Lerer, '*Forbidden Planet* and the Terrors of Philology', p. 83.

[35] Buchanan, *Shakespeare on Film*, pp. 155–6 and 154.

[36] Miller, '"In this last tempest"', p. 31.

The Korean War ended in 1953, the same year as the execution of the Rosenbergs for atomic espionage and just three years before the release of *Forbidden Planet*. The political introspection caused by McCarthyism and the sociological inspections inspired by this perception of material well-being and conformity might well give an impression of an externally confident but inwardly uncertain people. Surveying some of the contemporary critiques of that society, Temperley and Bradbury have written that "never had a people possessed so much in worldly goods, or, apparently, been so troubled in spirit on that account".[37]

To some extent the film offers a celebration of commodity culture: Robby's head looks strangely like a cash register and even lights up, and there is a comfortably comic exchange between Robby and Alta: 'Would diamonds or emeralds do?' 'Well, if they're large enough'. Robby is 'a housewife's dream', not only because he does the work, but also because he saves on the cost of ingredients, which he can reproduce in any quantity; when he arrives on Earth he will presumably disseminate this benefit there too.

This also raises some disturbing issues. Adams may say that Robby is 'a housewife's dream', but the cook wonders whether Robby is male or female, and Robby's response – 'In my case, sir, the question is totally without meaning' – despite its echoes of Ariel is hardly reassuring. In one sense the question answers itself, since, as Tim Youngs points out, 'Robby performs those domestic tasks which – especially in 1950s America – had been identified as women's duties', something which Youngs sees as ideologically sinister: 'The equivalence between women's and Robby's roles reinforces ideas of female servitude and therefore of man's mastery

[37] Youngs, 'Cruising against the Id', p. 219.

over machines and women'.[38] However, the film is not in fact fully confident that women can be safely kept in servitude and passivity. Although female desire is constructed as entirely responsive, Alta is an instinctive flirt. (Notably, she is made significantly older and more mature than Miranda: we hear 'Nineteen years ago' not 'Twelve years since', making the heroine 19 rather than nearly 15 years old.) In one sense, Alta has none of Miranda's knowledge of or pre-conceptions about sex; nevertheless, she says with instinctive provocativeness that 'I'm so glad you don't have any fire in *your* eyes, Lieutenant', to which the flustered lieutenant can respond only 'Well, I'm not *that* harmless'. In classic Mills and Boon fashion, the spark between Alta and the Captain is accompanied by aggression and dislike: he curtly informs her 'You can't run around like that in front of men', while the men resent the fact that they think the Captain is going to see Alta – so much so that one gives a sarcastic 'Aye aye, *sir*'. When Lt Farman says of kissing that 'You can't be in tiptop health without it', the deception, however innocent, further serves to mark sexual relations as something of a battlefield, an idea further underlined when Morbius informs the Captain and Farman that 'Sometimes the gauges register when the buck deer fight'.

Along with this queasiness about female sexuality and the possession of women in particular, there is also a profound unease about how ownership in general is to be established and protected. Simone Caroti sees the film as reflecting

The American 1950s, the decade of Doris Day, Sandra Dee, Elvis The Young and the USA as policeman of the world, where the sun of rationality and moral righteousness always shone,

---

[38] Youngs, 'Cruising against the Id', pp. 224 and 225.

> everybody was affluent and happy, and problems were something that lasted a couple of hours' viewing time and were never really serious to begin with.[39]

However, Sara Martin points out that '(the film) was released just a month after *Invasion of the Body Snatchers* (Don Siegel, 1956) in the midst of a decade marked by the Cold War and fears of secret invasions'.[40] This leads to a dark undertone of authoritarianism. As Anthony Miller observes, 'Authority in this Cold-War context is thus taken out of the hands of the dangerously unpredictable man of learning and entrusted to the reliable military man';[41] and Peter Biskind similarly comments that '*Forbidden Planet* is a conservative film in which the scientist has to make way for the soldier, in which technology, apparently, has gone too far',[42] while Tony Howard simply says that 'This kitsch, beautiful, film is politically reactionary – the intellectual must be distrusted and military force is benign'.[43]

Particularly suggestive is that the Captain works out the solution to the problem despite not having taken the brain booster. This is an interesting moment because it reveals a fundamental ambivalence not only to the brain booster, but also, more crucially, to what it represents. As Seth Lerer points out,

[39] Caroti, 'Science Fiction, *Forbidden Planet*, and Shakespeare's *The Tempest*'.

[40] Martin, 'Classic Shakespeare for All', p. 40.

[41] Miller, '"In this last tempest"', p. 32.

[42] Peter Biskind, *Seeing is Believing: How Hollywood Taught us to Stop Worrying and Love the Fifties* (London: Pluto Press, 1983), p. 109.

[43] Tony Howard, 'Shakespeare's Cinematic Offshoots', in *The Cambridge Companion to Shakespeare on Film*, edited by Russell Jackson (Cambridge: Cambridge University Press, 2000), pp. 295–313, p. 307.

Debates on measurable intelligence were at the heart of 1950s notions of society and education ... From the 1920s on, IQ became the marker of admission to the country – a device for separating out desirable and undesirable aliens, a supposedly quantifiable assessment of the quality of immigrant potential (and, in particular, of central European immigrant potential).[44]

However, there is also clearly a profound suspicion attaching to the overly intellectual, with Morbius as a prime example, so it is unsurprising that the Captain's unenhanced brain proves quite adequate. The ideal man should, it seems, be clever, but not too clever: Morbius's IQ is 183 and the doctor's 161, but the Captain's 'Maybe if we reason with him' turns out to mean shoot him, and when Morbius remarks that 'A commanding officer doesn't need brains, just a good loud voice' he may not be far from the truth. This is a marked reversal of the priorities of *The Tempest* itself, where Prospero's wisdom allows him to achieve all he wants and where Ferdinand is delighted to have found 'So rare a wondered father and a wise' (IV.i.123).

An equally big departure from *The Tempest* is the influence of psychoanalysis, and particularly of Freud. This emphasis too can be seen as part of the film's conservative politics. As Peter Biskind comments, 'Although conservatives repudiated it in principle, Freudianism was close enough to their own traditional Christian pessimism about human nature for them to find it serviceable',[45] as seen when Adams says 'We're all part monsters in our subconscious. So we have laws and religion'. Certainly Freudianism functions as a discourse of authority in *Forbidden Planet*. Anthony Miller argues that

[44] Lerer, '*Forbidden Planet* and the Terrors of Philology', p. 76.
[45] Biskind, *Seeing Is Believing*, p. 110.

The rebellion theme of Shakespeare's *Tempest* is excluded from the film; the crew of the spaceship contains no greater threat than a couple of irresponsible but apolitical wastrels. The Commander of the spaceship incorporates much of the authority that in Shakespeare belongs to Prospero. This authority includes the insight of the Freudian psychoanalyst, with its power to conduct Morbius to an understanding of his unconsciously motivated actions.[46]

Ironically, though, Freud's own authority does not pass entirely unchallenged in the film, because Jung too seems to be a presence. Michael Clifton describes Morbius summoning up the image of Alta as 'a projection of his own anima'[47] (as Morbius so suggestively says, 'I'll choose a familiar subject to start with, to save time'), and Sara Martin suggests that 'The colonial discourse is implicit here as in most science fiction and, arguably, *The Tempest*, but it is left aside in favour of self-consciously Freudian – perhaps, properly, Jungian – motifs'.[48] What Morbius describes as having happened to him in the Krell laboratory can also be compared to electroconvulsive therapy, first introduced in 1938 for schizophrenic patients and by 1940 part of the training given to US army doctors.

Whatever the precise nature of the explanatory model invoked to make sense of it, though, the world of the unconscious is undoubtedly a crucial force in *Forbidden Planet*. The monster that destroyed the crew of the *Bellerophon* and now threatens the

[46] Miller, '"In this last tempest"', p. 31.
[47] Michael Clifton, 'Cinematic Aliens: Moving Toward the Child', in *Genre at the Crossroads: The Challenge of Fantasy*, edited by George Slusser and Jean-Pierre Barricelli (Riverside, CA: Xenos Books, 2003), pp. 158–166, p. 160.
[48] Martin, 'Classic Shakespeare for All', p. 39.

modern crew is clearly intimately connected with sleep: as Adams says, in an attempt to reassert control of the situation, 'I'll have less dreaming aboard this ship'. Later Morbius says to Adams, 'I dare say neither of us slept last night', while the innocent Alta could earlier afford to say that she doesn't care whether she sleeps or not. Morbius says 'In nightmares I seem to feel the creature is waiting close at hand', and when an invisible force enters the ship, one of the crewmen senses it in a dream, though the unimpressed Captain exclaims 'A *dream!*' and punishes the dreamer with 20 extra watches. Although Adams insists that 'Hypnotic illusions don't tear people apart', when Morbius has a premonition of the attack, the audience surely has a premonition of their own about what is soon to be revealed: that not only does the machine work by brain power, but so too does the monster. This is first hinted at when the doctor speaks of 'Monsters from the id' and then dies, and is confirmed when Morbius explains the workings of the id. As the Captain comments, 'Even in you, the loving father, there still exists the mindless primitive'; indeed, though Morbius has a kind of psychomachia, it is a very uneven one and winning it kills him, suggesting that the evil within him is stronger than the good.

This is at least partly because the film has an id of its own, which it is hesitant about exploring openly. It is, after all, now Morbius and Alta who are structurally Adam and Eve (and Alta is *very* Eve-like, exhibiting the same kind of vain, flirtatious behaviour as Milton's Eve), despite the obvious counterclaim staked by Adams's name. There is furthermore at least a hint, as so often in versions of *The Tempest*, that when Morbius says 'Man is unfit as yet to receive such knowledge', he may be speaking personally (after all, he has a pretty terrifying id). Morbius, unlike Prospero, did not plan the arrival of a prospective suitor for Miranda, and the fact that Altaira is called after Altair slyly suggests *her* as the forbidden planet of the film's title. Although, as Judith Buchanan points out, 'contemporary reviewers missed the intimations of an incestuous relationship between Morbius and his daughter',[49] subsequent critics rarely have: Merrell Knighten, for instance, refers to 'the scientist Dr Morbius and his daughter Altaira, played with an Electral affection by Walter Pidgeon and Anne Francis',[50] while Peter Biskind declares that 'The only fly in the Oedipal ointment is the mysterious "planetary force" that tore the members of the first expedition limb from limb'. However it is, as Biskind also points out, 'the Skipper who answers the riddle of the planetary force', and thus in a further instance of competition for rôles, fulfils a different function of Oedipus from an earlier stage of the myth: that of solving the riddle of the Sphinx.[51] This tension between explanatory models is not entirely resolved by the completely unforeshadowed exchange which starts off as a plea from Alta to Morbius but ends as something quite different:

(Alta) 'Father ... Oh, father.'
(Morbius) 'Son – turn that disc. The switch – throw it.'

Since throwing the switch involves an extraordinary phallic-looking object, there is clearly a transfer of patriarchal power here in which Morbius acknowledges Adams as his legitimate successor as possessor of Altaira and, by extension, of Altair. Thus the film forecloses on its most troubling possibility and at least attempts to banish its own id at the same time as Morbius banishes his.

[49] Buchanan, 'Forbidden Planet and the Retrospective Attribution of Intentions', p. 152.
[50] Knighten, 'The Triple Paternity of Forbidden Planet', p. 36.
[51] Biskind, Seeing is Believing, pp. 108 and 110.

Whatever *Forbidden Planet* may have meant originally, it is now very much the product of the meanings that have accrued to it during the half-century since it was made. Though MGM's trade advertisement for the film began 'See an electronic blaster vaporize an attacking tiger in mid-air! See an invisible demon hurl an Earthman to fiery destruction!' and continued along similar lines, the special effects have not worn well.[52] The film has the now familiar trappings of countless space movies and series, except that the special effects look much more antiquated and slow; in particular, there is a hilariously unrealistic planet surface. Today, one of the principal impressions created by *Forbidden Planet* is of an earlier and cruder version of *Star Trek*, especially given the buddy-pairing of the Captain and the doctor (indeed Gene Roddenberry, creator of *Star Trek*, acknowledged the influence of the earlier film on his work). It even includes a typically *Star Trek* gag about who looks strange to whom when Alta thinks that the three are 'exceptions' to the normal run of Earth people, while when Robby the Robot says 'If you do not speak English, I am at your disposal with 187 other languages along with their various dialects and sub-tongues', we note not only the estrangement of English but also the anticipation of R2D2 in the *Star Trek*-influenced *Star Wars* films – especially since Alta later watches the destruction of her home planet, foreshadowing Princess Leia. And when Morbius says '... not even if I were the mad scientist ...', this is now experienced as a nod in passing to countless other offerings from the genre. Most notable, as Sara Martin points out, is the fact that '*Forbidden Planet* ignores the plot of treason to focus instead on the issue of monstrosity',[53]

[52] The full advertisement is quoted in Buchanan, '*Forbidden Planet* and the Retrospective Attribution of Intentions', p. 159.
[53] Martin, 'Classic Shakespeare for All', p. 40.

aligning it with an entire stable of monster movies. It is thus little wonder that the film's status as an adaptation of *The Tempest* is still marginal rather than canonical; when our institutional librarian offered to arrange screenings of all the Shakespearean texts we were teaching if we would choose the versions, he was appalled when I asked for *Forbidden Planet* for the week on *The Tempest*, and sent me an agonised email asking me to choose 'something respectable' like the BBC Shakespeare instead. And yet *Forbidden Planet* is an adaptation in the truest sense; tapping directly into some of the key concerns of its original, it reinvents and re-energises them, giving us in the process something rich and strange.

the tempest
(dir. Derek Jarman, (1979)

••

Derek Jarman might have made *Prospero's Books*. Not only does Jarman's Prospero dream the words of the opening scene – making his the only voice heard, in the same way as Gielgud's is in *Prospero's Books* – but Jarman also notes in his autobiography, *Dancing Ledge*, that when he first started thinking about *The Tempest* in 1975, Prospero would have been 'a schizophrenic locked into a madhouse – Bedlam. He plays all the parts' and 'I chatted with John Gielgud for a whole evening about it'.¹ It must therefore have rankled when Gielgud eventually made the film with Greenaway instead – 'While working with Greenaway on *A TV Dante*, Gielgud presented to him the idea of filming *The Tempest* with himself as Prospero, an idea which he had nourished for several years and which he had already suggested to Bergman, Kurosawa, and Fellini, among others'² – especially since Jarman had shared some of his ideas with Gielgud:

¹ Derek Jarman, *Dancing Ledge*, edited by Shaun Allen (London: Quartet Books, 1984), p. 140.

² Claus Schatz-Jacobsen, '"Knowing I Lov'd My Books": Shakespeare, Greenaway, and the Prosperous Dialectics of Word and Image', in *Screen Shakespeare*, edited by Michael Skovmand (Aarhus: Aarhus University Press, 1994), pp. 132–147, p. 133.

At first I made designs for an imaginary production at the Roundhouse, in which most of the theatre space was flooded, with the audience on a magic island of inflatable silver rocks, trampolines, and a huge, banner-like cloak. I talked with John Gielgud about these designs when we worked on the ill-starred production of *Don Giovanni*.[3]

Indeed Michael Anderegg declares simply that 'Greenaway was undeniably influenced by Jarman's film',[4] and although Judith Buchanan stresses the difference between the two films, observing that 'It seems that, consciously or otherwise, Greenaway picked up the baton from Jarman on some of the options he chose not to pursue',[5] there is a savage irony hovering over the account of Tristan Davies, a journalist quoted by Kate Chedgzoy, of how 'sitting in his shack surrounded by pebbles, plants and other exotica (Jarman) could almost have been the model for Peter Greenaway's Prospero'.[6]

In fact, the two directors are now generally construed as opposites. There were one or two awkward, albeit indirect, encounters between the two, one of which is noted by David Gardner:

When Peter Greenaway turned down a project for Italian television, Jarman's friend, Nico, proposed him instead:

I rang the producer and suggested you knew far more about history than Greenaway and could do his series; they told me they

[3] Jarman, *Dancing Ledge*, p. 183.

[4] Michael Anderegg, *Cinematic Shakespeare* (Lanham, MD: Rowman & Littlefield, 2004), p. 199.

[5] Judith Buchanan, *Shakespeare on Film* (Longman: Pearson, 2005), p. 174.

[6] Kate Chedgzoy, *Shakespeare's Queer Children: Sexual Politics and Contemporary Culture* (Manchester: Manchester University Press, 1995), p. 197.

wanted someone who had the reputation of being controversial but was safe. You I'm afraid they saw as just controversial.[7]

In *Being Naked Playing Dead: The Art of Peter Greenaway*, Alan Woods remarks of Jarman and Greenaway that 'There does not appear ... to have been any mutual sympathy between the two',[8] and Jarman himself says of Greenaway's *The Draughtsman's Contract* that 'It's the upstairs without the downstairs of independent films ... On the whole I liked the film; it was over-designed but nicely shot. I didn't care for the acting but this was compensated by the countryside (...) I thought the drawings were atrocious. They certainly were not seventeenth-century and were pretty absmal art-school stuff'.[9] Most notably, Kate Chedgzoy argues that 'Greenaway's deeply reactionary film is the antithesis of Jarman's *Tempest*'.[10]

Despite his own non-conformist reputation and the contrast now generally drawn between this film and *Prospero's Books*, Jarman's *Tempest* is in many ways traditional: indeed, as Rowland Wymer points out, Jarman identified to some extent with Shakespeare, seeing him as a fellow queer artist: 'An important aspect of this identification with Shakespeare was that Jarman saw both Shakespeare and himself as "conservative" and backward-looking artists, and thus representative of a general English cultural tendency'.[11] Though Kenneth Rothwell observes of the opening that 'The "split"

---

[7] David Gardner, 'Perverse law: Jarman as gay criminal hero', in *By Angels Driven: The Films of Derek Jarman*, edited by Chris Lippard (Trowbridge: Flicks Books, 1996), pp. 31–64, p. 59.

[8] Woods, *Being Naked Playing Dead*, p. 13.

[9] Jarman, *Dancing Ledge*, p. 25.

[10] Chedgzoy, *Shakespeare's Queer Children*, p. 198.

[11] Rowland Wymer, *Derek Jarman* (Manchester: Manchester University Press, 2005), p. 71.

acts as metaphor for Prospero's own desperate struggle against the alienation of self from self and society, as well as self-referentially Jarman's own split from conventional movie-making',[12] Jarman himself calls the film 'fairly conventional', though he compares it with the implied blandness of Branagh. For one thing, it was not entirely a break with all previous ideas about ways of filming *The Tempest*: Judith Buchanan observes that 'In the same year, 1979, that Powell told *Film Comment* that he had still not "wholly abandoned" his plan to make a film of *The Tempest*, Derek Jarman, an admirer of Powell's work, went into production with his own low-budget version of the play, suggesting in interview later that the project had in some sense been "inherited" from Powell'.[13] For another, it paid great respect to Shakespeare. The opening credits announce the film as 'William Shakespeare's *The Tempest*' and follow Shakespeare almost slavishly in introducing Caliban as 'a savage and deformed slave' and Ariel as 'an airy spirit'. Jarman even notes that there was a portrait of Elizabeth of Bohemia, at whose 1613 wedding Shakespeare's play was performed, in the hall of the house which he refers to as their 'island' – Stoneleigh Abbey in Warwickshire.[14] The house takes on a particular prominence in this film because shooting took place in midwinter so that the Abbey was covered in snow, limiting the possibility of outdoor scenes. As a result the house becomes virtually a character in its own right.

Less conventional in Shakespearean terms, though very much more so within the history of film, is the fact that the psychological

[12] Kenneth S. Rothwell, *A History of Shakespeare on Screen*, 2nd edition (Cambridge: Cambridge University Press, 2004), p. 196.

[13] Judith Buchanan, *Shakespeare on Film* (Longman: Pearson, 2005), p. 159.

[14] Jarman, *Dancing Ledge*, p. 188.

is the dominant mode of explanation in this film. In Rowland Wymer's words, 'At the centre of Jarman's film is the psychological journey of a figure who is simultaneously Dee, Prospero, Shakespeare, and Jarman himself'.[15] As Kate Chedgzoy notes, 'The earliest notes for a possible film of *The Tempest* can be found in a notebook dating from the autumn of 1974, which would make the entire thing a psychodrama enacted within the mind of a Prospero maddened by delusions of power and obsessive attention to cabalistic studies'; originally Prospero was going to voice a puppet-like Ariel and Miranda, and Prospero himself was going to be in a madhouse.[16] Although this idea was ultimately abandoned, the idea of sleep and dreams remains central throughout:

> The repreated cries of "We split! We split!" enact a nightmare of psychic disintegration rather than showing Prospero as in full magical control of the storm scene. At times, the bedchamber itself takes on the same monochrome look as the ship at sea, eroding the distinction between dreamer and dream.[17]

Prospero has his eyes closed at both the beginning and the end of the film. The last words are 'Our little life is rounded with a sleep', spoken over an immobile Prospero, so that 'sleep' stands in the place of prominence occupied by 'free' in the original text. Ariel is not seen at first, so he could be in Prospero's head; and the fact that the opening scene is dreamed by Prospero, before we cut to Miranda, may well suggest that she is at least as much an inhabitant of Prospero's mind as a real person. Indeed Judith

[15] Wymer, *Derek Jarman*, p. 76.

[16] Chedgzoy, *Shakespeare's Queer Children*, p. 197.

[17] Wymer, *Derek Jarman*, p. 77.

Buchanan has argued that 'Since the whole action is to be seen as emanating from the unconscious mind of the dreamer, Prospero, the film therefore deliberately offers itself as an insight into the workings of that mind'.[18]

Jarman himself observed that 'For *The Tempest* we needed an island of the mind, that opened mysteriously like Chinese boxes',[19] and there are a number of indications of a psychologising perspective: Caliban pronounces Sycorax as 'Psychorax', though Prospero does not, and this Sycorax presides over a realm without clothes or boundaries, suggestive of the semiotic. In contrast to this fluidity, Prospero's world is one of the mirror, the prop which Jacques Lacan has associated with the transition away from the semiotic and into the symbolic. Ferdinand shows Miranda her reflection in a mirror at the top of Prospero's staff (which was, as Rowland Wymer points out, 'topped by a modified version of Dee's Hieroglyphic Monad');[20] Ariel seems to appear in a mirror to give his report, and later rehearses 'Let me remember thee what thou hast promised me' in the mirror; subsequently, Prospero imprisons Ariel in the mirror.

Perhaps an inevitable effect of this emphasis on the psyche is that the relationship between Prospero and Miranda is presented as both strongly hierarchical and also subtly unsettling. Toyah Wilcox's is an unusually ambiguous Miranda, who has polarised critical opinion. Though Kenneth Rothwell declares that 'The characters have been audaciously displaced into a contemporary mold, the boldest stroke being the re-invention of Miranda (Toyah Willcox) as a voluptuous tart, a "nymphomaniac" to use Jarman's

[18] Buchanan, *Shakespeare on Film*, p. 160.

[19] Jarman, *Dancing Ledge*, p. 186.

[20] Wymer, *Derek Jarman*, p. 76.

own label',[21] Susan Bennett suggests that casting Toyah Wilcox has some positive effects in that it makes Miranda more visible, because Wilcox was so closely identified with punk:

> Connected to a movement whose identification was with aberrant, often violent social behaviors as a rejection of mainstream values, her body (as the primary site for her designation as a punk artist) works against the romanticization of Miranda and against the apparent naturalness of the match with Ferdinand.[22]

Equally Jim Ellis suggests that 'Miranda is in general given far more agency in this film than in other versions, and her tiny rebellions against her father are given more prominence'.[23] However, Russell Jackson observes that

> Miranda ... has clearly been kept in childishness well beyond the time of physical maturing: there is no self-conscious eroticism in her behaviour, but her body speaks for itself, and the child's fantasy world is established deftly in such scenes as that in which she stands on a rocking-horse, thinking the lines of the masque.[24]

[21] Rothwell, *A History of Shakespeare on Screen*, p. 197.

[22] Susan Bennett, *Performing Nostalgia: Shifting Shakespeare and the Contemporary Past* (London: Routledge, 1996), p. 132.

[23] Jim Ellis, 'Conjuring *The Tempest*: Derek Jarman and the Spectacle of Redemption', *GLQ* 7.2 (2001), pp. 265–84, p. 271.

[24] Russell Jackson, 'Shakespeare's Comedies on Film', in *Shakespeare and the Moving Image: The Plays on Film and Television*, edited by Anthony Davies and Stanley Wells (Cambridge: Cambridge University Press, 1994), pp. 99–120, p. 108.

There is a similar split in the ways In which the film invites us to view her. Heathcote Williams's young, active Prospero is not a particularly paternal figure, and his relationship with his daughter is uneasy. It is notable that Prospero holds a sword under Antonio's eye, which clearly has Oedipal overtones, since Oedipus puts out his own eyes on learning about his involuntary incest with his mother. He also comes running into Miranda's bedroom where she is in bed to deliver the 'A devil, a born devil ...' speech in a way which we may well perceive as sinister. It is difficult in these circumstances to construe their relationship as a healthy one.

However much she may be the focus of Prospero's interest, however, Miranda is not the primary draw for the camera. As Jim Ellis points out,

> It is Ferdinand's rather than Miranda's body that is offered to the viewer as erotic spectacle, as Ferdinand stumbles naked from the waves like a homoerotic Venus, wanders across the dunes, and then decorously falls asleep by a fireplace in Prospero's home. By contrast Miranda's partial nakedness leaves her neither vulnerable nor a sexual object; the scene of her vigorously scrubbing herself by the fire is notably unerotic.[25]

This serves to estrange the viewer's perspective from Prospero's: since we look at Ferdinand while Prospero looks at Miranda, his gaze, which would usually pass unnoticed in the heternormative conventions of mainstream cinema, here comes to seem perverse and idiosyncratic. The effect is reinforced by the way in which Caliban 'functions as a caricature of heterosexual male desire, helplessly slavering over the inaccessible Miranda, alternatively

[25] Ellis, 'Conjuring *The Tempest*', p. 271.

contemplating rape and shrinking back in cowardly terror', while 'The heterosexual union of Ferdinand and Miranda, which would conventionally represent the moment of narrative closure and resolution, takes place within an absurdist parody of Shakespeare's masque'.[26] David Hawkes argues that this is central to the overall narrative thrust of the adaptation, which 'precludes any sympathetic identification with Prospero, and complicates the classical narrative form, which generally presents the male protagonist as an ego-ideal for the viewer'.[27] Indeed Chantal Zabus and Kevin A. Dwyer see Jarman's as an essentially Gothic film with a frighteningly out-of-control Prospero from whom the audience is inevitably wholly alienated,[28] and William Pencak points out that on Prospero's desk is a bust of Mausolus, builder of 'the world's largest and most elaborate tomb'.[29] This may chime with the fact that the film is dedicated 'to the memory of Elizabeth Evelyn Jarman', the director's mother, and the solemnity evoked by the obvious fact of a death here is underlined by the fact that there is no music at the end. What is emphasised is loss and absence, rather than celebration or integration.

In keeping with the film's emphasis on the psychological, there is little sense of the real in Jarman's *Tempest*: as Rowland Wymer observes of Jarman's approach in this film, 'His own settings can hardly be called naturalistic but he was extremely anxious that they should neither conflict with the poetry nor merely "illustrate"

---

[26] David Hawkes, '"The shadow of this time": the Renaissance cinema of Derek Jarman', in *By Angels Driven: The Films of Derek Jarman*, edited by Chris Lippard (Trowbridge: Flicks Books, 1996), pp. 103–116, pp. 108–9.

[27] Hawkes, '"The shadow of this time"', p. 108.

[28] Zabus and Dwyer, '"I'll be wise hereafter"', p. 277.

[29] William Pencak, *The Films of Derek Jarman* (Jefferson, NC: McFarland & Co, 2002), p. 107.

it, but allow "the verse to breathe"'.[30] When filming scenes in the vicinity of Bamburgh Castle, all the beach scenes were shot through a blue filter, which makes the scenes resemble twilight and so heightens the impression of a time of dreams; indeed Jarman records his pleasure that 'The blue filters worked. I was desperately anxious that the exteriors should not look real, and chose the dunes at Bamburgh for their lack of features'.[31] Kenneth Rothwell notes that

> In an early draft of his plans, Jarman himself anticipated that "stylistically the film will take great freedom" and it will be "in black-and-white, shot like a German expressionist horror film (*Nosferatu*)," but at at the end it "will burst into radiant color," though he must have changed his mind because the final cut emerged in color throughout. The exterior scenes with a blue filtered lighting may possibly have been inspired by Caravaggio's hallmark *tenebrism*, that is to say, muted contrasts between white and black.[32]

However, a less painterly and more psychologising explanation is also clearly possible. William Pencak suggests that

> All the film's outdoor scenes are a sickly blue, a color Jarman later used in his final film, *Blue*, to depict the void seen by the blind, and which he also used sparingly to depict disease and death in *Caravaggio*, citing the painter's supposed remark that the color blue was "poison." At the same time, the indoor scenes

[30] Wymer, *Derek Jarman*, p. 72.

[31] Jarman, *Dancing Ledge*, p. 203.

[32] Rothwell, *A History of Shakespeare on Screen*, p. 196.

effect the alchemical transformation Agrippa's work discusses: earth colors (browns and reds) are transformed through fire into gold.[33]

There are also other alchemical elements in the film: Rowland Wymer argues that

Caliban's slavering enjoyment in sucking raw eggs appears to exemplify his "gross" and "earthy" nature but there is one remarkable shot of him lifting an egg to his mouth where the egg is briefly silhouetted against the flames behind him, creating a powerful alchemic emblem. It is also significant that the candles on the floor of Prospero's cell appear to be arranged in the shape of a bird.[34]

As Wymer points out,

Jarman's interest in alchemy and Renaissance occult philosophy had been prompted by his readings of Jung who, rather than dismissing these things as pre-scientific aberrations, had interpreted the alchemists' preoccupation with material and spiritual transmutation and their search for a lost unity in psychological terms.[35]

Equally Jim Ellis notes that 'Prospero consults the copy of Agrippa's *Occult Philosophy* that was owned by Jarman, and Prospero has on his staff a reproduction of Dee's "hieroglyph

[33] Pencak, *The Films of Derek Jarman*, pp. 102–3.

[34] Wymer, *Derek Jarman*, p. 77.

[35] Wymer, *Derek Jarman*, p. 77.

monas"'. Ellis further suggests that 'Alchemy becomes for Jarman an analogy for his own cinematic art as well as for queer filmmakers' and that 'The entrance of the sailors draws on a more contemporary discourse, camp. Camp is perhaps the modern equivalent of alchemy, practised by a marginalized group, dependent upon a specialized knowledge, and representative of an entire philosophical outlook'.[36] Even without assuming such an equivalence, however, a reference to alchemy is highly appropriate in the film of *The Tempest* because there is such a strong underlay of alchemical allusion in the original play: 'In Shakespeare's time, the term "tempest" represented "the alchemical term for the boiling of the alembic to remove impurities and transform the base metal into purest gold"'.[37]

As well as the use of non-naturalistic colour effects, other factors militate against any sense of realism in the film. Ferdinand chops wood in the living room, and there is a really improbable number of candles burning while Prospero begins his long speech (here dislocated until after Sebastian's and Antonio's attempt has been foiled and Ferdinand set to log-work, around 25 minutes in). Equally, however, there is a paradoxical minimisation of the artificial. Despite Jarman's assertion that '*The Tempest* is a masque; what it lacks, in the theatre productions I've seen, is a sense of fun',[38] and Sara Martin's comment that '*The Tempest*, Jarman insisted, is a masque – a view Greenaway also sustains',[39] there is none of the mannerism of the masque genre. There is also little humour, and

[36] Ellis, 'Conjuring *The Tempest*', pp. 277–8.

[37] Simone Caroti, 'Science Fiction, *Forbidden Planet*, and Shakespeare's *The Tempest*', *Comparative Literature and Culture* 6.1 (March, 2004). Online: http://clcwebjournal.lib.purdue.edu/clcweb04-1/caroti04.html

[38] Jarman, *Dancing Ledge*, p. 203.

[39] Martin, 'Classic Shakespeare for All', p. 37.

little interest in realising the magical elements of the narrative other than the suggestion, already noted, of the alchemical, which essentially depends on an idea of organic transformation rather than showy effect. Stephano and Trinculo encounter Caliban together rather than separately, and the business is cut; Jarman's view is that 'we were able to jettison the cruder theatrical magic of the stage for something more refined and developed'.[40] It is true that Kenneth Rothwell does detect a trace of residual magic, since he suggests that 'Stephano and Trinculo remain "simple and ordinary people," in fact filmed as characters from *The Wizard of Oz* happily skipping along a beach';[41] moreover, as Steven Dillon points out, 'Jarman notably cuts out those lines where Prospero promises to break his staff and drown his books, and this can only give the impression that Prospero's magic continues and that poetry is not destroyed'.[42] Nevertheless, this is not where the film's energies lie.

Rather than in the magic, this film is interested in its characters. Particularly striking is Jarman's Caliban: bald, shabbily dressed, and acted by a blind performer, he eats an egg in its shell, giggles insanely, and has a northern accent and bad teeth. Most of all, he is very childlike. Although 'Early plans for the film had included a black, beautiful, sympathetic Caliban, wearing a mother-of-pearl necklace to symbolise the loveliness of the world he had shared with Sycorax, and a green and red costume associating him with the elements of earth and fire', the Caliban eventually cast was very different. As Kate Chedgzoy points out,

[40] Jarman, *Dancing Ledge*, p. 190.

[41] Rothwell, *A History of Shakespeare on Screen*, p. 196.

[42] Steven Dillon, *Derek Jarman and Lyric Film* (Texas: University of Texas Press, 2004), p. 90.

The film's Caliban, Jack Birkett, is a dancer and mime artiste who had worked with the Lindsay Kemp company and also had his own drag act. Casting decisions of this kind may well have helped to draw in people who would not normally think of themselves as Shakespeareans, but must also have exacerbated the anxieties of a more conservative potential audience.[43]

Her point is neatly illustrated by Kenneth Rothwell's very different terms for much the same information: 'Caliban, played by the perennial favorite of the Lindsay Kemp clique, The Incredible Orlando (Jack Birkett) of Titania fame, is a giggling obnoxious satyr who resembles Lindsay Kemp's Puck in the Coronado *Midsummer Night's Dream*'.[44] Rothwell's ire is aroused particularly by the scene in which we see Caliban with his mother, with 'the adult Caliban suckling greedily at her breast, in a formal tableau which deliberately constructs a perverse parody of a "Madonna and child" painting'.[45]

The allusion to paintings detected by Rothwell is something that will, of course, be shared with Jarman; and just as Jarman's *Tempest* is in some ways more traditional than might have been expected, so it actually has more in common with the adaptation with which it is so often contrasted. Douglas Lanier lists a number of similarities between *Prospero's Books* and Jarman's *Tempest*, although he also suggests a major difference: 'Jarman interrogates content, Greenaway form'.[46] Equally, Steven Dillon points to the

[43] Chedgzoy, *Shakespeare's Queer Children*, pp. 202 and 196.

[44] Rothwell, *A History of Shakespeare on Screen*, p. 197.

[45] Chedgzoy, *Shakespeare's Queer Children*, p. 202.

[46] Douglas Lanier, 'Drowning the Book: *Prospero's Books* and the Textual Shakespeare', in *Shakespeare on Film: Contemporary Critical Essays*, edited by Robert Shaughnessy (Basingstoke: Palgrave, 1998), pp. 173–195, p. 182. On what Greenaway and Jarman have in common biographically, see Orr, 'The Art of National Identity', p. 329.

importance of water – a key motif for both directors: 'Choosing to film *The Tempest* allows Jarman to immerse himself once again in watery imagery'.[47] Both Jarman's *Tempest* and Greenaway's *Prospero's Books* share a lot more nakedness, and a lot less sense of an island, than are offered in the original play; both, too, are interested in horses. In Jarman's film, Ariel delivers the marriage-blessing to Miranda while riding on a rocking-horse, before she has even met Ferdinand; later, when she has, she stands on the rocking-horse and remembers it. Rowland Wymer observes that 'One of the film's key properties is a rocking-horse, which signifies that Miranda has not entirely left the nursery but which, as in D H Lawrence's short story "The Rocking Horse Winner", starts to become highly sexualised'.[48] The same motif is evoked again later, when fairground music plays in the background as Ferdinand is being given clothes. There is also an impulse both in Jarman's *Tempest* and in *Prospero's Books* to harness Shakespeare to ends other than simple admiration for the play; to that extent, both adaptations might well be termed parasitic rather than realisatory. Finally, both directors were interested in architecture; indeed Niklaus Pevsner was one of Jarman's tutors,[49] and in Jarman's *Tempest*, as later in Greenaway's, there is careful attention to the details of the Renaissance. The 'frippery' here is masks, vaguely reminiscent of Venetian carnival masks, and in Jarman's original plan the set and Prospero's own appearance were going to be closely modelled on Renaissance paintings.

However, as in Jarman's *Edward II* (a film linked to this by the fact that Jarman's niece, Kate Temple, played the young Miranda and was a seamstress on *Edward II*), these things are important not only

[47] Dillon, *Derek Jarman and Lyric Film*, p. 91.

[48] Wymer, *Derek Jarman*, p. 78.

[49] Jarman, *Dancing Ledge*, p. 69.

as images but also as symbols of power. Antonio is a Cardinal who blesses the sword before Sebastian raises it against the king, suggesting an unholy alliance of church and state and giving the play the same implicitly anti-ecclesiastical agenda as *Edward II*. The sound of marching feet, audible over Prospero's depiction of how he and Miranda were put in the boat, adds an anti-military feel. It is notable, too, that Gonzalo delivers the commonwealth speech with the castle, emblem of feudal power, looming behind him. Against these symbols of the state apparatus, humans are represented as distinctly disempowered: the 'harpies' are a freak show – dwarves, who later help Miranda dress for her wedding – and although all the other Neapolitans land fully clothed, Ferdinand lands naked and arrives at Bamburgh Castle still in that state of vulnerability and exposure, until Prospero eventually issues him with white clothes. Prospero alone exerts power.

Moreover, a central point about Jarman's *Tempest* is the extent to which it is conceived as a sequel to his *Jubilee* (1977) – an ironic vision of Britain which we are afforded when John Dee says to Elizabeth I, 'Sweet majesty, pluck up thy heart and be merry, for I will reveal to thee the shadow of this time', upon which we cut to punk, post-industrial Brtiain with a burning pram and graffiti saying 'postmodern'. There is a considerable casting overlap between the two films: Toyah Wilcox is Miranda in *The Tempest* and Mad in *Jubilee*; Jack Birkett is Caliban in *The Tempest* and Borgia Ginz in *Jubilee*; Karl Johnson is Ariel in *The Tempest* and Sphinx in *Jubilee*. *Jubilee* also ends with the words 'Come away', and the name of John Dee's angel (David Brandon, credited as David Haughton) is changed to Ariel and he is given lines from Shakespeare's Ariel; the two films share an interest in alchemy, full-frontal nudity, and a notably sparse soundtrack. The visual style is also similar: *Jubilee* opens in a dark, candle-lit country house much like the one in which *The Tempest* is set, and the dwarf who attends on Elizabeth I reappears at the wedding of Ferdinand and Miranda. Again this is visibly 'poor film': the queen's pearls are obviously false, and the film offers a troubled meditation from Amyl Nitrite on art as a substitute for life in times when the pursuit of desire and dreams was forbidden (with Amyl Nitrite classing Myra Hindley as an artist). Together, *Jubilee* and *The Tempest* can be seen as effectively a diptych about who holds power in Britain today and the extent to which they derive it from the past (a *topos* which *Edward II* was to develop further.)

Nevertheless, although he came from a family of India hands and lived there himself as a child,[50] Jarman has little interest in the power dynamic that modern criticism has found most interesting for analysis of *The Tempest*. Nor does he offer anything that could resemble a postcolonial reading of the play – even though, as Rowland Wymer observes, colonialist readings, though relatively newly emergent in the UK, were already well established in the US.[51] Indeed, Kate Chedgzoy declares that

Jarman explicitly eschewed the interest in colonialism which has loomed so large in reproductions of *The Tempest* in recent decades, telling one interviewer, "it was very possible to make Caliban black, but I rejected it because I thought it would load the whole film in one way, make it more specific rather than general" ... Jarman's phrasing here reproduces a racist paradigm which sets whiteness up as neutral and universal, blackness as a "marked", deviant condition.[52]

[50] Jarman, *Dancing Ledge*, pp. 46–7.

[51] Wymer, *Derek Jarman*, p. 73.

[52] Chedgzoy, *Shakespeare's Queer Children*, p. 202.

Instead, the dynamic in which Jarman's film is interested is much more personal, and centres principally on Prospero and Ariel. Ariel is experienced first as a voice in Prospero's head before being seen as a wasted, white-clad figure with very expressionless, flat delivery. He could stand for an emblem of Death, and plays with an animal skull in white-gloved hands. Jarman himself commented:

> Our Prospero is young and healthy, the first time he has been cast that way; beside him Ariel seems wan, world-weary. It's a subtle reversal of the accepted order. Most of the lines are there: (not) 'Do you love me master no?' – we've cut that out as with my reputation they'd expect it. Karl plays his part deadpan. He's in the most modern of our costumes, which are a chronology of the 350 years of the play's existence, like the patina on old bronze.[53]

It is true that youth and health were not the only reasons for the casting of Heathcote Williams. Although he was so inexperienced that Jarman actually had to obtain an Equity card for him, he was a member of the Magic Circle,[54] and Kate Chedgzoy observes that

> Jarman possessed a substantial collection of books on magic, and the details of magical practices represented in the film are all drawn from his own research into the Elizabethan esoteric tradition. Heathcote Williams was cast as Prospero because he shared the film's interest in the occult to the extent of being skilled in practical magic himself.[55]

[53] Jarman, *Dancing Ledge*, p. 196.
[54] Buchanan, *Shakespeare on Film*, p. 160.
[55] Chedgzoy, *Shakespeare's Queer Children*, p. 200.

Whatever its initial motivation, however, the casting of Heathcote Williams also brought with it other resonances. The tension between a Prospero who is well and an Ariel who is not offers a powerful demarcation, and one which was to take on savage resonance after Jarman himself was diagnosed with AIDS. Indeed, as Rowland Wymer points out, 'shortly after Jarman's HIV positive diagnosis in 1986, he deliberately broke "Prospero's wand, Dee's hieroglyphic monad"'.[56] Though that had not yet happened when he made *The Tempest* – the disease was only just beginning to be talked about – health and faculties (especially in the context of Birkett's blindness) here stand as a privilege which some possess and others do not. They will function in the same way in Jarman's later *oeuvre*, making it an expression of power dynamics no less resonant for not being explicitly post-colonial. Jarman's version of *The Tempest* may not be one which Shakespeare would have recognised, but it is one which has spoken loudly to its own time.

[56] Wymer, *Derek Jarman*, p. 80.

prospero's books
(dir. Peter Greenaway, 1991)

....

Prospero's Books is a film about a book which repeatedly pits the idea of books against the idea of film: as Geoffrey Wall comments, '*This Tempest* is mainly about the pleasures and the anxieties of representation'.[1] Martin Butler observes that

> Books fill its *mise-en-scène*, either as texts that Prospero writes or as props for the action. Cast adrift at sea, the infant Miranda wears a hat folded from a printed leaf; during the rebellion in Milan, scholars in the library mop up blood with loose paper; Prospero remembers his wife as a beautiful corpse, her head cradled on the open pages of a great folio.[2]

In one of the earliest shots, we see 'Boatswain' written as Prospero says 'Bo'sun', something which Greenaway himself calls

[1] Geoffrey Wall, 'Greenaway Filming *The Tempest*', *Shakespeare Yearbook* 4 (1994), pp. 335–9, p. 335.

[2] Martin Butler, 'Prospero in Cyberspace', in *Re-constructing the Book: Literary texts in transmission*, edited by Maureen Bell, Shirley Chew, Simon Eliot, Lynette Hunter and James L. W. West III (Aldershot: Ashgate, 2002), pp. 184–196, p. 185.

'a nice opening point about the topsy-turvy use of oral and written language'.[3] As Alan Woods comments of Greenaway in general, 'It is a visual habit he has, to set an image of a word beside an image of what it names'; Greenaway himself recalls that 'In 1981 I wrote a script called *Jonson and Jones* which sounds as if it ought to be set in Chicago, perhaps in the 1920s, but it refers to the partnership and quarrels of Ben Jonson and Inigo Jones in the making of Jacobean court masques',[4] and on a different occasion added that 'I suppose it's my rewriting of the Michael Nyman/Peter Greenaway relationship'.[5] The cause of the celebrated quarrel between Inigo Jones and Ben Jonson was a dispute over whether the words or the stage picture was the more important, with Jonson maintaining that 'the masque has two parts: one, which is addressed to the understanding, is the soul; the other, which is addressed to the senses, is the body'.[6] Although Greenaway never

[3] Adam Barker, 'A Tale of Two Magicians', in *Film/Literature/Heritage: A Sight and Sound Reader*, edited by Ginette Vincendeau (London: British Film Institute, 2001), pp. 109–115, p. 111. For comment on this shot, see also Amy Lawrence, *The Films of Peter Greenaway* (Cambridge: Cambridge University Press, 1997), pp. 140–1, and Claus Schatz-Jacobsen, '"Knowing I Lov'd My Books": Shakespeare, Greenaway, and the Prosperous Dialectics of Word and Image', in *Screen Shakespeare*, edited by Michael Skovmand (Aarhus: Aarhus University Press, 1994), pp. 132–147, p. 142.

[4] Alan Woods, *Being Naked Playing Dead: The Art of Peter Greenaway* (Manchester: Manchester University Press, 1996), pp. 113 and 238.

[5] Christel Stalpaert, 'The Artistic Creative Process, its Mythologising Effect and its Apparent Naturalness Called into Question: An Interview with Peter Greenaway', in *Peter Greenaway's Prospero's Books: Critical Essays*, edited by Christel Stalpaert (Ghent: Academia Press, 2000), pp. 27–41, p. 41.

[6] D. J. Gordon, 'Poet and Architect: The Intellectual Setting of the Quarrel between Ben Jonson and Inigo Jones', in *The Renaissance Imagination: Essays and Lectures by D. J. Gordon*, edited by Stephen Orgel (Berkeley: University of California Press, 1975), pp. 77–101, p. 79.

made this film, the oppositions it would have addressed are central to *Prospero's Books*.

For H. R. Coursen, Greenaway's use of these oppositions is ultimately counter-productive: 'It is a film in which two "contents" – Shakespeare's script and the books that Peter Greenaway invents for Prospero – compete with each other. The effect is not "irony," but incoherence'.[7] Equally, though, the tension could be seen as an energising one, encouraging comment rather than competition. This is a film in which it is never possible to forget the effect of representational mode on perception; as such, it not only develops an idea already implicit in Shakespeare's text, but also adds a new dimension. As Douglas Lanier points out of the 'Boatswain' shot,

> The handwriting even features visual puns – the "I" of the word "sail" is, for example, drawn as a ship's mast – all of which tend to draw attention to the text's visual look, its status as a visual object, rather than to its meaning. More important, by reframing the text in this manner, Greenaway acknowledges his desire to be faithful to it while dismantling its received monumentality and authority.[8]

One of the defining conceits of Shakespeare's *Tempest* is the way in which it pits a first scene focused entirely on the visual and on sound effects with a second focused entirely on verbal narrative and scene-painting, with the verbal ultimately triumphing as Prospero assures Miranda that all the elaborate effects she has just seen have been merely so much illusion. To this already established

---

[7] H. R. Coursen, *Watching Shakespeare on Television* (London and Toronto: Associated University Presses, 1993), p. 163.

[8] Lanier, 'Drowning the Book: *Prospero's Books* and the Textual Shakespeare', p. 183.

tension between the shown and the spoken, Greenaway adds an extra layer – that of the written. This also stands for the fact that his text, rather than speaking freshly to the audience as Shakespeare's play did (an effect all the more marked because unusually, Shakespeare was working without a source text here), must always work through the medium of Shakespeare's pre-existing text.

Even further prominence is given to the written by the fact that, as Thomas P. Brockelman describes,

> First of all, a video image is overlaid upon the surface of the film, partially (but almost never entirely) covering the represented action "behind" it. One sees, for example, the book of water "framed," as it were, by the edges of a shot of Prospero in his bathhouse. Then, within the insets by which each of the magical books is described, Greenaway presents sequences that follow the logic of the "magical book" in making the text constantly give way to what it "represents": the book of water proves to be wet, the book of motions shakes upon its shelf. At these moments, the inset tends to expand, taking up the entire screen. But, as the inset narrative winds to its end, Greenaway shrinks the video image again, using the distancing devices of picture framing and sometimes affixing an actual gilded picture frame to it.[9]

Even more startlingly, as Brockelman observes, 'In concluding the victorious resolution scene of *The Tempest*, the director actually scrapes the physical surface of the film upon which the scene is represented, insisting through this unique gesture upon our

[9] Thomas P. Brockelman, *The Frame and the Mirror: On Collage and the Postmodern* (Evanston: Northwestern University Press, 2001), p. 79.

perception of it as a filmic text',[10] while James Andreas points out that 'The horizontal tracking of film is based on the methodology of writing and reading so brilliantly recreated in the incessant procession of John Gielgud from screen left to right in *Prospero's Books*'.[11]

Equally, however, we are never allowed to forget that the written is only one element in the equation. We are invited to register the full force of the difference between the spoken and written words not only through pronunciation, but also because the writing is so stylised: 'I know how to CURSE', for instance, is clearly not, as might be expected, taken from the First Folio, but is written in a mocked-up (and unnaturally legible) version of a 17th-century hand. As Martin Butler comments, 'the letter-forms are not taken from the 16th-century secretary hand which Shakespeare himself wrote, since they would have been undecipherable to a 20th-century cinema audience'. Butler goes on to observe that 'As for the written text, its status is curiously ambiguous. It is not a theatrical manuscript, as the screenplay seems to predict, for it bears none of the customary signs of playhouse use'; ultimately, he suggests, 'the film further blurs the distinction between the written and printed word by avoiding any reference to the mechanics of printing'.[12] In fact,

[10] Brockelman, *The Frame and the Mirror*, p. 83.

[11] James Andreas, '"Where's the Master?": The Technologies of the Stage, Book, and Screen in *The Tempest* and *Prospero's Books*', in *Shakespeare Without Class: Misappropriations of Cultural Capital*, edited by Donald K. Hedrick and Bryan Reynolds (Basingstoke: Palgrave, 2000), pp. 189–208, p. 200.

[12] Martin Butler, 'Prospero in Cyberspace', in *Re-constructing the Book: Literary texts in transmission*, edited by Maureen Bell, Shirley Chew, Simon Eliot, Lynette Hunter and James L. W. West III (Aldershot: Ashgate, 2002), pp. 184–196, pp. 195, n. 3, 187, and 188.

Brody Neuenschwander created the calligraphy for the film, working with Greenaway's direction to produce a hand that retained an authentic Renaissance script while at the same time revealing a seventeenth-century decadence. Greenaway wanted an excessive calligraphy that would capture the meaning of the words, their sound patterns and literary associations.[13]

It is true that 'In one voyage ...' *does* look like the First Folio; certainly the books destroyed include Leonardo and the First Folio, though Caliban rescues the latter. However, 'WOULD BECOME TENDER' is clearly written in capitals and repeated merely for emphasis rather than in any attempt to reproduce original typographical features. The effect is thus one of an informed and fundamentally playful engagement with the differences between the written and spoken forms of these words.

The books motif of the film also suggests the range of know-ledges on which the play draws, and the range of ideas which it generates. This is especially marked as pieces of paper fly past Caliban, Stephano and Trinculo, indicating the extent to which their social marginalisation is based on their exclusion from a community that is conditioned by the ideas disseminated through literacy. However, as Lia M. Hotchkiss points out,

Prospero ... seems to treat many books cavalierly as well. During his voyage to the isle, he lets the toddler Miranda play with a book, and torn pages form a paper hat for her to wear. He

---

[13] M. E. Warlick, 'Art, Allegory and Alchemy in Peter Greenaway's Prospero's Books', in New Directions in Emblem Studies, edited by Amy Wygant (Glasgow: Glasgow Emblem Studies, 1999), pp. 109–136, p. 114.

leaves an ink bottle to spill its contents on the trembling *Book of Motion*. During the tempest modeled on the isle, books are either rained or urinated on.[14]

This mishandling of books even by the élite (on which the film is of course fundamentally predicated, since it itself 'mishandles' a classic text) goes hand in hand with evidence of a widespread distrust of language. Significantly, two of the few lines cut by Greenaway are 'Your tale, sir, would cure deafness' and 'Well demanded, wench', both of which testify to the power of speech and its ability to command attention and evoke a response. There is also an (admittedly rare) misrendition – 'pluck your highness' frown upon you', instead of 'his highness' – which went uncaught, as if no one had really been listening to the words. Judith Buchanan further notes that Gielgud says 'mountain air' instead of 'mountain winds'; she argues that 'In this film, in which every image and effect is carefully contained and controlled, it is legitimate to read every adjustment, however slight, as in some way strategic', but it is of course equally possible that the details of the words are not what is considered important here.[15]

Certainly if words and images are at odds, it is images that win. Particularly notable in this respect is that after all the ingenuity of the language games at the opening, the epilogue has no tricks –

[14] Lia M. Hotchkiss, 'The Incorporation of Word as Image in Peter Greenaway's *Prospero's Books*', in *The Reel Shakespeare: Alternative Cinema and Theory*, edited by Lisa S Starks and Courtney Lehmann (Cranbury, NJ: Associated University Presses, 2002), pp. 95–117, p. 110.

[15] Judith Buchanan, 'Cantankerous Scholars and the Production of a Canonical Text: The Appropriation of Hieronymite Space in *Prospero's Books*', in *Peter Greenaway's Prospero's Books: Critical Essays*, edited by Christel Stalpaert (Ghent: Academia Press, 2000), pp. 43–85, p. 48.

just Gielgud's face speaking and then retreating. Obviously this represents Prospero's renunciation of his art, but it also and analogously signals a precisely similar 'renunciation' on Greenaway's part, and a simple trust in the communicative power of the unadorned image. On 'free', water gushes; Ariel runs forward, there is fire and water, and the onstage audience claps. Ariel's running goes into slow-motion as he heads straight for the camera and flies out of shot and out of language. This is in striking contrast to Prospero, who on 'free' is confined within a box, as if Greenaway's brand of freedom were superior to his; Chris Lawson argues that at the end of the film 'Gielgud essentially becomes trapped within the filmic frame, shrinking into the distance as the black borders of the frame steadily encroach on either side ... both Prospero and Gielgud are shown to be manipulated and consumed by their environment, being reduced to the subject of a painting: a framed, two-dimensional enigma'.[16] Greenaway may graciously cede centre stage throughout the film to Gielgud's alternative brand of magery and image-making, but ultimately his own superiority is neatly implied.

Thus, if the film about Jones and Jonson had ever been made, it is not hard to guess that Jones would have triumphed – indeed Michael Anderegg declares that '*Prospero's Books* is an homage to both Shakespeare and Inigo Jones, or at least the spirit of Inigo Jones' –[17] for Greenaway trusts more to images than to words.

[16] Chris Lawson, 'The Greenwayan Sensory Experience: The Interdependency of Image, Music, Text and Voice as Interconnected Networks of Knowledge and Experience', in *Peter Greenaway's Prospero's Books: Critical Essays*, edited by Christel Stalpaert (Ghent: Academia Press, 2000), pp. 141–159, p. 143.
[17] Michael Anderegg, *Cinematic Shakespeare* (Lanham, MD: Rowman & Littlefield, 2004), p. 194.

Caliban is a dancer, communicating through movement rather than speech; Prospero may speak his lines, but Caliban can still convey meaning. Like Jarman's, this film is particularly fond of mirrors: there is a book of mirrors, of which Eckart Voigts-Virchow comments that

> While the encyclopedic knowledge of texts serve(s) Prospero as a source of his world, he also needs mirror-images to realize his visions, which makes his *Book of Mirrors* the essential device in his imaginings, working both temporally and spatially ... His mirror also enables him to view his enemies all over the island.[18]

It is notable, though, that the mirror functions on strictly intra-diegetic terms, rather than reaching out to disturb or even inflect the film's relationship with its audience. As Herbert Klein points out,

> (Ariel) confronts Prospero with the result of his actions by holding up three mirror images to give Prospero insight into his own deeds and bring about a change in him. The first image portrays Alonzo as a father bowed down with grief kneeling by his dead son, the second image portrays Ferdinand feeling both humiliated and intimidated, and the third picture shows the trio Caliban, Stephano and Trinculo driven to flight in a state of disgrace.[19]

[18] Eckart Voigts-Virchow, 'Something richer, stranger, more self-indulgent: Peter Greenaway's Fantastic See-Changes in *Prospero's Books* et al', in *Anglistik und Englischunterricht* 59 (1996), pp. 8399, p. 91.

[19] Herbert Klein, "The far side of the mirror": Peter Greenaway's *Prospero's Books*', *Erfurt Electronic Studies in English* (1996).
Online: http://webdoc.sub.gwdg.de/edoc/ia/eese/eese.html

Once again, then, Greenaway's image-making works to contain the power of Prospero at the same time as producing it. Mirrors are held up around Prospero for the cloud-capped towers speech, and then curtains close behind him; as M. E. Warlick observes,

> Picture frames, mirrors and other rectilinear frames are used to enclose images of the past and distant present. These frames and mirrors are often carried by nude figures of all shapes and sizes, unaltered by the artist's idealizing hand. They recall the painted illusionist figures found in abundance in Renaissance and Baroque ceilings, naturalistic nudes and *grisaille* imitations of sculptures who linger at the outer edges of framed narrative scenes. These mirrors become devices to 'hold' the image. Those who hold these mirrors carry additional symbolic weight, reflecting both optimistic and pessimistic moods, underscored by the postures, ages, beauty and skin colours of their nude carriers.[20]

Paradoxically, though, this proliferation of mirrors ultimately renders the surface of the film invisible. In a direct inversion of the scratching which elsewhere draws our attention to that very surface, here the medium itself dissolves from sight, becoming a transparent window which both effaces and affirms the power of Greenaway's auteurship.

Other sources of visual imagery form repeated patterns in the film. As well as actual mirrors, another reflective substance, water, 'being the source of Greenaway's obsessions',[21] is also important

[20] Warlick, 'Art, Allegory and Alchemy in Peter Greenaway's *Prospero's Books*', p. 117.

[21] Zabus and Dwyer, "'I'll be wise hereafter'", p. 282.

throughout;[22] Eckart Voigts-Virchow notes that 'In an interview Greenaway has stated that he "tried to find as many characters as (he) could who had an allegorical reference to water"', and observes that 'Water is arguably the most pervasive area of imagery in Greenaway's movies'.[23] Thus the first thing we see is water dropping and then water intercut with writing, summing up neatly the repeated juxtapositions to come of images of the natural and images of the cultural (which in turn play on a raw/cooked polarity – a recurrent feature of Greenaway's work).

Horses are also important. Miranda is first seen with a horse in the background, and horses surround her and Ferdinand as they pledge love. To some extent, this is perhaps simply because the horses in this film contrast so strongly with the mixed species prominent elsewhere – Caliban, himself identified as the 'offspring of bestiality', steals a book about the Minotaur –[24] but it is also noteworthy that Greenaway at one stage projected a film entirely based on paintings of horses.[25] At times even the books seem to exist as much for the image they present as for their intellectual content: '*All knowledge is erotic to the desirous. In this particular library, though the sexual organs are primarily masculine, the vaginal creases of the interior spine of the books and the billowing curves of the pages themselves are indubitably feminine*'.[26]

[22] On the ubiquitousness of water in Greenaway's *oeuvre* in general, see Laura Denham, *The Films of Peter Greenaway* (London: Minerva Press, 1993), p. 37.

[23] Voigts-Virchow, 'Something richer, stranger, more self-indulgent', pp. 92 and 93.

[24] Greenaway, *Prospero's Books*, pp. 21 and 95.

[25] Denham, *The Films of Peter Greenaway*, p. 39. For comment on Greenaway's interest in horses, see also Woods, *Being Naked Playing Dead*, pp. 174 ff.

[26] Leon Steinmetz and Peter Greenaway, *The World of Peter Greenaway* (Boston: Journey Editions, 1995), pp. 112–3.

We must make what we can of these pictures, because Greenaway is not generally a helpful explicator of his own work. Adam Barker notes that 'When asked to consider the personal roots of his work, Greenaway is at first unexpectedly reticent, and then skilfully guides the conversation back to safer ground';[27] although the last of the film credits – Director Peter Greenaway – stands alone, Greenaway the director/auteur/magician is ironically anxious to hide, seeking to become even more invisible than the surface of his film. In the book which accompanies the film, Greenaway says slyly, 'Since the reading of scripts can be tedious, there is some evidence that it is written to be entertaining'; he also refers to 'its ambition', as if it were nothing to do with him,[28] and says, 'perhaps it is a collection of lost da Vinci drawings',[29] maintaining the fiction that the books are lost to him too. However, it is undoubtedly revealing that the accompanying book for this project, *Prospero's Subjects*, consists entirely of still photos,[30] and strongly draws attention to the following:

In the film *Prospero's Books*, John Gielgud, playing Prospero in Shakespeare's *The Tempest*, colonizes his island with creatures. Shakespeare does not elaborate about this island population. We do. Some of his island subjects are native, some are immigrants, some magic-ed out of thin air. Using them all as raw material, Prospero invents, discovers, and creates a court that masquerades as a theater of the world. The film is full of these creatures – accommodating Prospero's expectations, littering his palaces, over-spilling his staircases, and populating his

[27] Barker, 'A Tale of Two Magicians', p. 110.

[28] Peter Greenaway, *Prospero's Books: A Film of Shakespeare's* The Tempest (London: Chatto & Windus, 1991), p. 12.

[29] Greenaway, *Prospero's Books*, p. 39.

[30] Peter Greenaway, *Prospero's Subjects* (Kamakura: Yobisha Co Ltd, 1992).

bedrooms. Being no slouch for symbolic intent, his audiences are also allegories fulfilling emblematic purposes – butcher, Mars, architect, politician, ambassador, Venus, gardener, scholar, St Agatha, ink mistress, iconoclast. They follow an honourable tradition – like Chaucer's archetypes, like the characters writ large in the very title of *The Cook, The Thief, His Wife and Her Lover* – they are both types and ciphers, understandable according to the characteristics of their employment – but they are also, beneath the cipher, idiosyncratic humans needing all the personality traits to flesh them out into believability.

Such was my unfinished fascination for these creatures in the film, that I expanded on them – and began to write a fuller account of their purposes. Perhaps this new text may become a novel. Or a film.[31]

Neither the novel nor the film ever materialised;[32] it was, clearly, the images that fired Greenaway's imagination. Even here, though, he hides, since at a crucial stage of this passage his authorial control is explicitly denied by that sly use of 'we'.

In typical Greenaway fashion, many of the images he uses grow directly out of the historical context proposed for the film. As soon as Amboise and the King of France (neither present in the original text) are mentioned, we know exactly what that context is: the Renaissance, as classically conceived (and, notably, a rather earlier stage of the Renaissance than that at which Shakespeare wrote his play). Again in typical Greenaway fashion, and as is

---

[31] Steinmetz and Greenaway, *The World of Peter Greenaway*, pp. 106–7.

[32] Laura Denham comments that *Prospero's Books* 'is meant as one of a trilogy', the other works being *Prospero's Creatures* and a play called *Miranda* about what happens on the ship home (Denham, *The Films of Peter Greenaway*, p. 39).

entirely consistent with his fascination for architecture,[33] the Renaissance is expressed primarily through its buildings. The film is set almost entirely within buildings, with a preponderance of classical ruins and indoor pools. Caliban, Stephano and Trinculo sit on a pile of yellow sand, but the effect is more of a building site than of a beach. The nearest we get to nature is a garden (which perhaps evokes reminscences of *The Draughtsman's Contract*); there is no sense of an island. Laura Denham comments that

> The island is built to fit the requirements of someone who misses Italy, and several of the buildings – the palace of libraries for example, which is faithfully copied from a Florentine architectural masterpiece by Michelangelo – are exact replicas. Sometimes, however, designs are based on work of a far later period than the early 1600s ... The dubious justification for this aberration is that Prospero is a magician and therefore has supernatural foresight. Similarly the fact that the shipwrecked Neapolitans look as though they have stepped out of a Rembrandt is tenuously excused because Naples had strong dynastic connections with the Spanish Netherlands.[34]

Earlier buildings are also evoked: Prospero's bath-house is based on the Great Mosque at Cordoba,[35] and what goes on in it looks a bit like a Roman orgy.

[33] Laura Denham comments that 'The role of "art"... as an organising tool and part of a figurative, intellectual language instead of as a decorative appendage, is elsewhere fulfilled by Architecture' (*The Films of Peter Greenaway*, p. 18).

[34] Denham, *The Films of Peter Greenaway*, p. 41. See also Greenaway, *Prospero's Books*, p. 108.

[35] See Warlick, 'Art, Allegory and Alchemy in Peter Greenaway's *Prospero's Books*', p. 112.

As well as buildings, clothes are also important, and the tension between clothes and nakedness provides a recurring motif in the film, analogous to that between nature and the written. There are naked women with long blonde hair, suggestive of Rhinemaidens, who buffet the tiny ship, and before Caliban is seen there are images of pages with unpleasant liquids and suspicious-looking solids dropped on them, suggesting his unrestrained physicality; when he does appear, the point is further emphasised by the fact that he is naked, and we see a flashback to him as a child. Douglas Lanier, arguing that `*Prospero's Books* relentlessly draws our attention to performers' bodies; it converts Shakespearean narrative into non-narrative, non-verbal bodily forms', points out that `nearly all of Prospero's army of magical spirits are unclothed, a choice that the beleaguered Greenaway has defended in interviews as a homage to the idealised nude body of Renaissance art'.[36] Lanier himself supplies the defence that Greenaway cannot, when he claims that `his interest in nudity in this production is not thematic or prurient, but formal, that is, in the physical body as a medium'.[37] (Peggy Phelan neatly describes Prospero's threat to Ariel as essentially `you used to be a nobody, doing work you didn't want to, making those porn movies with Sycorax and with me you are a star doing good work and soon you will be able to work for yourself',[38] and Peter Donaldson notes that Prospero

[36] Michael Anderegg calls it 'At once an "art film" and something resembling soft-core pornography (these may, at times, seem to be the same thing)' (Anderegg, *Cinematic Shakespeare*, p. 191).

[37] Lanier, 'Drowning the Book: *Prospero's Books* and the Textual Shakespeare', pp. 186–7.

[38] Peggy Phelan, 'Numbering *Prospero's Books*', *Performing Arts Journal* 14.2 (1992), pp. 43–50, p. 49.

studiously ignores all the naked people,[39] defusing any suggestion that they are sexual, while Peter Schwenger more cautiously calls them 'equivocal, perhaps allegorical nudes'.)[40] Lanier also points out that bodies are important partly because of the way in which they are counterpoised with books: 'When Prospero imagines Antonio's *coup d'état*, he sees two conjoined waves of destruction, one of bloody bodies, the other of books'.[41] Moreover, the insistent nakedness allows for a particularly striking contrast with the clothes used in the film. Ferdinand in particular oscillates tellingly between swimming completely naked and wearing an elaborate hat, veil and ruff which are strongly reminiscent of the mannered visual style of *The Draughtsman's Contract*.

Ruffs are important elsewhere in the film too. The 'wardrobe' which Caliban, Stephano and Trinculo attempt to steal from Prospero consists entirely of ruffs; the Neapolitans are chased away by dogs in ruff-like collars; 'How beauteous mankind is' (V.i.183) is delivered to a convention of ruffs; and later we hear the words 'Heavens keep him from these beasts' (II.i.325) spoken over a shot of a ruffed dog. Nor are ruffs the only clothes which are emphasised. Tellingly, as Greenaway himself notes, Ariel at Prospero's prompting stands on the hem of Miranda's dress to show off her curves to Ferdinand.[42] Gielgud wears a doge's hat, and also

[39] Peter S. Donaldson, 'Shakespeare in the Age of Post-Mechanical Reproduction: Sexual and electronic magic in *Prospero's Books*', in *Shakespeare, the Movie: Popularizing the plays on film, TV, and video*, edited by Lynda E. Boose and Richard Burt (London: Routledge, 1997), pp. 169–185, p. 181.

[40] Peter Schwenger, 'Prospero's Books and the Visionary Page', *Textual Practice* 8.2 (summer 1994), pp. 268–78, p. 270.

[41] Lanier, 'Drowning the Book: *Prospero's Books* and the Textual Shakespeare', p. 188.

[42] Greenaway, *Prospero's Books*, p. 105.

appears above the harpies' feast (a cross between Harvest Festival and Arcimboldo) with Ariel on his lap, looking like a Pantocrator and wearing cerulean blue. Jonathan Romney interestingly comments that 'the only true precursor of this filmed Shakespeare is Max Reinhardt's 1935 *A Midsummer Night's Dream*, whose turbaned princeling is briefly reincarnated here by Ariel (another *Dream* echoed is Peter Brook's production, with its trapezes)'.[43] It is typical of Greenaway that the film should echo visual details of set and costume, rather than ideas.

It is one of the film's most powerful ironies that these clothed and civilised beings should be so profoundly bizarre. The women who tended Miranda, for instance, are horrors. The court is thronged with Rubensesque women with blank faces. Even Susanna, Prospero's wife, is not much brighter-looking and is entirely objectified by being turned into a living illustration of Vesalius' supposed banned, heretical 'second book on birth'. Chantal Zabus and Kevin A. Dwyer see this as picking up on a wider theme of the film as a whole: 'Prospero acts as a midwife to the pregnant Sycorax. He is the ultimate deliverer: he delivers Ariel from the cloven pine; and he "delivers" all the lines of the voiceless characters in the play'.[44] However, other critics have been less charitable and less willing to detect artistic control here. In particular, it makes for an odd effect when Prospero rather than Caliban says of the projected rape of Miranda, 'Oho. Would't had been done!', and though calligraphy and design both package

[43] Jonathan Romney, Review of *Prospero's Books*, in *Film/Literature/Heritage: A Sight and Sound Reader*, edited by Ginette Vincendeau (London: British Film Institute, 2001), pp. 142–5, p. 144.

[44] Zabus and Dwyer, "'I'll be wise hereafter'", p. 283.

> We split
>> We split
>>> We split

in the most controlled way possible, it is still notable that Prospero comes into Miranda's bedroom – as in Jarman, but unlike in other adaptations. (Here it is Miranda's sleep that is tormented, rather than Prospero's, as if in a deliberate inversion of Jarman.) Officially the stress is on cold, clinical artistic control, a cultured interplay with the source text, and meaningful juxtaposition of images, but together these particular images exceed their proposed meanings and raise some other, more disturbing questions. Greenaway does not seem to want to take account of these, at least some of which bear directly on the motivation and hidden desires of ageing male control freaks. It is therefore unsurprising that Geoffrey Wall asks sceptically, 'Greenaway is evidently fascinated by the mysterious mess of conception, pregnancy and birth. But what do they add up to, thematically, all these scenes of women bleeding?'.[45]

One of the things they might add up to, of course, is an obsession. Peter S. Donaldson, reading *Prospero's Books* in the context of interpretations of *The Tempest* which regard Prospero's magic as primarily concerned with controlling female sexuality, sees even Prospero's ultimate compassion as 'yet one more appropriation, or reappopriation, of the feminine'. Donaldson comments interestingly too on the extent to which computer technology such as that in which the film delights is gendered masculine, insinuating (even if he does not ultimately develop) something of a parallel between Greenaway and Prospero here.[46] Obsessions and abnormal

[45] Wall, 'Greenaway Filming *The Tempest*', p. 337.
[46] Donaldson, 'Shakespeare in the Age of Post-Mechanical Reproduction', pp. 176–7 and 173.

psychologies are certainly a recurrent feature of *Prospero's Books*, although the film does its best to suggest that it is in full control of them. This is, transparently, a society in collective need of psycho-analysis, and indeed a psychoanalytic approach is repeatedly suggested. The entire film is structured on the principle of voices being experienced in the head, as people either speak in unison or Prospero speaks their lines over them: writing projected over Ferdinand and Miranda suggests the extent to which their rôles are already inscribed. One inevitable result of this is a sharp flattening of affect: Geoffrey Wall declares that 'With Gielgud speaking everyone's lines for most of the time, we don't begin to care about the characters',[47] although, as Eckart Voigts-Virchow observes, this is not a phenomenon unique to *Prospero's Books* but rather a recurring feature of Greenaway's films:

> With the possible exception of Stourley Kracklite, individuality escapes Greenaway's characters. They are mere vessels that contain meanings. Standard psychoanalytic readings which see the fantastic as a visualization of the repressed are bound to fail, because Greenaway's fantasy subverts the cinematic identification process. He refuses to supply insights into the psychological make-up of characters, which instead reflect the culture at large.[48]

What is sharply marked in *Prospero's Books*, though, is the especial prominence of the idea of the dream, so crucial in psycho-analysis. Most notably, it is crucial in the presentation of Miranda, who just sleeps at first; the camera lingers on her asleep as Prospero

[47] Wall, 'Greenaway Filming *The Tempest*', p. 335.

[48] Voigts-Virchow, 'Something richer, stranger, more self-indulgent', p. 93.

says that he has 'made thee more profit than other princes(s) can' (I.ii.173). It is therefore unsurprising that, in keeping with the logic of a psychoanalytic approach, which traditionally regards human impulses as universal rather than culturally produced, the drive towards the transhistorical is almost as strong as the drive to contextualise. Particularly noticeable in this respect is the film's downplaying of the importance of the classical past, so important to the Renaissance (and found, as we have seen, even in *Forbidden Planet*.) There is a musical march at the beginning of where the masque should be, after which 'Hail many coloured messenger' is sung by a woman in a spectacular ruff. There is nothing remotely classical about this; someone crosses in front of the woman with a mandolin, and the masque becomes entirely music and spectacle. It is true that the classical content is to some extent displaced onto the image of the Minotaur and other beast/man crosses but essentially it is ignored. Indeed, far from directing us to the classical past, Greenaway darts all over the globe as the map and projection of the island include 'Aztec' golden fields of corn, a maze from Rheims Cathedral, and a 'Fire of London Monument'.[49]

In fact, for all its ostensible setting in the Renaissance, the film ranges widely in the periods that it evokes. Claribel's hairstyle is based on the wildly out-of-period Klimt,[50] and as Alan Woods comments, 'Caliban's island is a recreation of eighteenth-century English Shakespeare illustrations'.[51] Michael Anderegg remarks that 'Specifically, Greenaway is drawn to compositions inspired by European large canvases of the seventeenth and eighteenth

[49] Greenaway, *Prospero's Books*, pp. 6–7.

[50] Warlick, 'Art, Allegory and Alchemy in Peter Greenaway's *Prospero's Books*', p. 112.

[51] Woods, *Being Naked Playing Dead*, p. 85.

centuries: David, Rubens, Veronese',[52] while Laura Denham observes that 'Greenaway's staging of the Shakespearean text incorporates so many cinematic replications of historical paintings that a shot by shot account of the film reads something like the contents page of an art history book',[53] of which she lists several. (Amongst other references, Lia M. Hotchkiss points out that 'Miranda ... wears a sheer sprigged dress based on Botticelli's painting of Spring'.)[54] Amy Lawrence notes that as Prospero warns Ferdinand not to anticipate the wedding,

> A series of books appear, embodying references to Greek mythology in images borrowed from motion studies conducted by the nineteenth-century photographer Eadweard Muybridge. Greenaway recombines photographs from Muybridge's eleven-volume study *Animal Locomotion* (1885) to evoke what the narrator tells us are pornographic scenes from antiquity.[55]

Jonathan Romney sums it up:

> When a succession of spirits present wedding gifts to the young couple, each gift is only briefly glimpsed, but each is meticulously composed and lit to resemble a Dutch still life. Greenaway is no less profligate with his erudition, and the allusions to Renaissance Italian, Dutch Golden Age, Spanish and French nineteenth-century painting are legion.[56]

[52] Anderegg, *Cinematic Shakespeare*, p. 193.

[53] Denham, *The Films of Peter Greenaway*, p. 25.

[54] Hotchkiss, 'The Incorporation of Word as Image in Peter Greenaway's *Prospero's Books*', p. 96.

[55] Lawrence, *The Films of Peter Greenaway*, p. 158.

[56] Romney, Review of *Prospero's Books*, p. 144.

The film is, in short, a veritable collage of different periods and cultures.

The most striking result of its transhistorical perspective is the fact that Greenaway's film, like Jarman's, has no interest in a post-colonial reading nor indeed, despite the fact that it was released in the year of Desert Storm, in any other kind of politically aware reading. Greenaway writes in *Prospero's Books* that Ferdinand, whose 'body is white and not made for manual work', sorts white logs from black, but shows no sign of any sense of the ironies attendant here (so is it all right to assume that black people's bodies *are* made for manual work?). The island itself is 'perhaps off the north-west coast of Africa ... maybe further down the African coast ... perhaps further out still in the Atlantic ocean'. Chantal Zabus and Kevin A Dwyer offer a partly recuperative reading of the lack of any postcolonial awareness in the film:

> ... we know that Greenaway could easily have portrayed Caliban as a monstrosity, since he is known to create vile creatures, making use of grotesque bodies and images ... Caliban's traditional bestiality is here somewhat abated by his aquatic grace, which is Greenaway's way of rendering Caliban's poetic prowess in the original play.

However, even they concur that in *Prospero's Books* 'Caliban is presented as an abstraction, an Id of sorts, a mere presence to contrast with Miranda's, Ferdinand's and Ariel's purity and their higher training in the civilized arts'.[57]

Rather than a reading grounded in the history of colonialism, Greenaway goes for a universalising one, with the presence of 'four

[57] Zabus and Dwyer, "'I'll be wise hereafter'", p. 283 and 284.

Ariels to represent the elements'[58] clearly directing our attention towards nature rather than culture. There is certainly no hint of political correctness in the image of an African court in which we see 'an abused Claribel ... her backside bare and bleeding', nor is there much sensitivity to history in the simile which observes that the sailors from the wreck are 'lying like naked crusaders on their tombs'.[59] Although Prospero looks at some of the John White images from Roanoke while voicing Gonzalo's commonwealth speech, this glance at the real history of colonialism is notably absent elsewhere, and, as so often in these adaptations, the delivery of 'This thing of darkness I/Acknowledge mine' is, once again, flat and unemotional.

It is of a piece with this lack of questioning of Prospero and his actions that the other characters' points of view are consistently suppressed. As Herbert Klein points out, 'Miranda sees the images of her past (which she herself can no longer remember) through Prospero's eyes'.[60] As so often in Greenaway, women characters in particular are marginalised: as Peggy Phelan notes, 'Miranda seems like a mutely beautiful doll'.[61] There is no 'It is a villain, sir, I do not love to look on', an omission which chips away at any sense of Miranda as an autonomous individual, and Claribel too has her eyes closed and is downcast, while the reclining 'African' stares challengingly ahead: Greenaway may evince little to no interest in non-whites in this film, but even a non-white man, it seems, ranks higher than a woman. A particularly negative side of this flattening of character is the downplaying of any sense of conflict in the

[58] Greenaway, *Prospero's Books*, p. 12.
[59] Greenaway, *Prospero's Books*, pp. 121, 12, 114, and 185–6.
[60] Klein, '"The far side of the mirror": Peter Greenaway's *Prospero's Books*'.
[61] Phelan, 'Numbering *Prospero's Books*', p. 49.

narrative: as H. R. Coursen comments, 'Cupid is played by one of the Ariels, another erasure of tension, since Cupid in the masque mirrors the threat that Caliban represents in the outer play'.[62] The one perspective that remains, and dominates, is Prospero's. This is partly because for Greenaway, 'Prospero, omnipotent magician, inventor and manipulator of characters, can be conceivably appreciated as a Shakespearean self-portrait'[63] (and also, by implication, a Greenaway self-portrait). Consequently resistance to Prospero is systematically toned down: there is no 'Yes, Caliban her son', and no 'O my father! I have broke your hest to say so!'. Amy Lawrence points out that 'In the script, the captives, released from the spell, speak for themselves in scene 89 (out of 91). The result, though, does not so much liberate the characters, allowing them to speak as equals to Prospero, as it enables them to acknowledge his power more fully'.[64] She also argues that originally, masques incorporated a level of anxiety, and that

> Prospero unleashes the masques when his power is confirmed. Unfortunately, for a modern audience, the masques' utter lack of anxiety translates into a lack of suspense. The already high level of spectacle throughout the film makes the endless parade of extras decidedly anticlimactic.[65]

Eliminating the masque, therefore, silently positions the film as a seamless representation of power. In this version, the play is not

[62] Coursen, *Watching Shakespeare on Television*, p. 173.

[63] Greenaway, *Prospero's Books*, p. 9.

[64] Amy Lawrence, *The Films of Peter Greenaway* (Cambridge: Cambridge University Press, 1997), p. 148.

[65] Lawrence, *The Films of Peter Greenaway*, p. 162.

about cultural history or colonial metaphor: it is, as its title announces, about Prospero's books; all the other characters are merely supporting actors in that story. As such, it also becomes about Greenaway's books; and just as the film as a whole alternates between offering itself as transparent window and drawing our attention to scratches on its surface, so its control of its project does sometimes waver, troubling us with gaps and dark suggestions which seem ultimately to speak more of Greenaway than they do of Prospero.

conclusion

Considered collectively, these adaptations reveal a number of elements and moments in *The Tempest* which provide pivotal interpretative cruxes or can turn out to sound the keynote for an entire adaptation. Some of the ways in which film adaptations of *The Tempest* habitually work are predictable: it is perhaps inevitable that film, a distinctively modern medium, should consistently seek to downplay or ignore altogether the classical elements that were so important in the original play. Ironically, only the most futuristic adaptation of the play, *Forbidden Planet*, is really interested in these, though even here the Christianising 'The view looks just like heaven' stands in place of the classicising 'Most sure, the goddess'. There is nothing classical at all in Stow's film – indeed, the only allusion to mythology points entirely in the opposite direction, in the shape of the Viking longship that removes them from the island. Greenaway too pays far less attention to the classical world than to the Renaissance and even to some of the periods which follow it: there is no 'Most sure, the goddess' here either, and the *Book of Mythologies,* which immediately precedes the masque, covers material 'from the icy north to the deserts of Africa' rather than focusing on Greece and Rome. Ironically, the only purely classical book in *Prospero's Books* is *The Autobiographies of Pasiphaë and Semiramis*.

Perhaps the biggest surprise in this respect is Mazursky's *Tempest*, because although Kalibanos calls Miranda 'beautiful goddess' and is a bit like Polyphemus, and despite a (very fleeting) shot of the Parthenon, the idea of Greek heritage turns out to be largely a red herring. There is a hilarious exchange about the cultural meanings of Greece, in which its attractions are listed: these start with the Parthenon and culminate in Telly Savalas. A similarly jokey tone is apparent when Phillip says of the casino, 'We name the dining rooms after the gods' and when Dolores, the Gonzalo character, falls for Kalibanos and tells him 'You're so strong, so beautifully ... primitive'; 'You have charisma'. In fact the true Greek, Kalibanos, lives entirely by the jingles and clichés of other cultures: he shows Miranda 'Gunsmoke' on his TV, and sings 'Double your pleasure, double your fun' as he watches her swim.

Both Bender's *The Tempest* and the *Animated Tales* version shed all sense of the classical past; although one harpy in the *Animated Tales* is boucephalic, this is clearly incidental rather than programmatic. In Jarman's version Elisabeth Welch is billed as a goddess, but the director himself declares that 'Single-handed, she replaced Iris, Ceres and Juno'.[1] Judith Buchanan offers an ingenious argument for the very absence of classical detailing in Jarman as functioning as all the more profound a reminder of the classical world – 'Jarman's uncostumed presentation of Ariel as the harpy reminds us that it is the conscience of the beholders that makes a harpy of the voice of accusation',[2] revealing to us the extent to which their imagination is so steeped in classical images that it

---

[1] Jarman, *Dancing Ledge*, p. 191.

[2] Judith Buchanan, *Shakespeare on Film* (Longman: Pearson, 2005), p. 161.

produces them even when they are not physically there – but by the same token it also underlines the extent to which a modern audience does not see in terms of the classical past.

Nor is it surprising that film should generally ignore the play's adherence to the classical unities – Mazursky's *Tempest* pointedly takes place within one day (we cut from the mountain to 'New York ... 18 months earlier'), and Jarman's may do so, but both abundantly compensate for observation of the unity of time by violation of the unity of place. It is an inevitable part of *Forbidden Planet*'s take on the play that a night should need to pass, and Bender's *The Tempest* clearly unfolds over a period of years, while in Stow, a caption explicitly tells us that it is 'Ten years later'. *Prospero's Books* does not visibly violate the unity of time, but there is an excursus to Tunis, and the film's many allusions to art and buildings from a wide range of periods mean that we are principally aware of chronological diversity rather than chronological unity.

It is even less surprising that film should struggle with the masque form. Although Judith Buchanan does suggest of *Prospero's Books* that 'the whole film feels more like an extended masque than a drama in which the sequence of action matters crucially', the masque proper is invariably replaced or, as in *Prospero's Books*, handled obliquely.[3] Conversely, it is equally unsurprising that many of these adaptations should find the magical elements congenial, though in fact there is perhaps less emphasis on these than might have been expected. Russell Jackson observes that

Derek Jarman's film of *The Tempest* ... uses very little of the trick technology of the cinema ... it is the work of an image-maker. There are no flying effects or glass shots, and the most elaborate

[3] Buchanan, *Shakespeare on Film*, p. 177.

optical effects are those used to present the image of Ariel in a mirror over a fireplace or the sight of scenes and characters through the magic glass on Prospero's staff ... the film has plenty of extraordinary visions, but they are produced for the most part by staging tableaux and filming them.[4]

Indeed the hunt scene in the Jarman is the filmic equivalent of poor theatre: as Judith Buchanan notes,

In both the harpy scene and the scene of the hounding with dogs Jarman exploits his audience's understanding of how theatrical as opposed to cinematic illusions typically work, in order to alert them to a deliberate self-limitation in his cinematic style at this point.

Buchanan comments of Jarman's *Tempest* in general that 'the magic in the film is much more noticeable for its elaborate processes than for its achievements'.[5] Bender's film does include some magical sequences and is very interested in the spells and incantations which Gideon Prosper performs, but in *Forbidden Planet* magic has been replaced by psychic forces and technology in more or less equal parts (though Morbius does call his steel shutters 'a bit of parlour magic'). In Greenaway, intradiegetic magic plays second fiddle to the extradiegetic technological wizardry: ineed Michael Anderegg declares that 'Apart from the precise nature of the technology involved, many of the magical moments in *Prospero's Books* might have been achieved by

[4] Jackson, 'Shakespeare's Comedies on Film', p. 107.

[5] Buchanan, *Shakespeare on Film*, pp. 163 and 161.

George Méliès circa 1905'.[6] In Mazursky, the very notion of magic seems defused when Aretha refers to 'storms and electrical appliances'; the doctor says 'I'm not a magician', and Phillip calls himself 'the king of high tech'. However, in a way Aretha helps Phillip and Miranda become invisible; there are lots of effects for the storm; and Phillip, after repeatedly saying 'Show me the magic', finally does magic with his glasses to raise the tempest – though how he is able to do this is never explained. It is as if no version of *The Tempest* can entirely relinquish the magic elements; nevertheless, only the *Animated Tales* version, in which Prospero's robe and collar come on by magic, showcases them.

There is also less use made of music than might have been expected. Although in *Requiem for Methuselah* – the episode of *Star Trek* based on *Forbidden Planet* – Flint has been, amongst other famous figures from history, Johannes Brahms, and Aretha in *Tempest* is a singer, adaptations have not generally engaged in any imaginative way with the noises that haunt the isle. *Forbidden Planet* itself offers electronic noises rather than music, and even when Morbius plays Krell music it is not too dissimilar from the soundtrack. In the *Animated Tales*, music is first heard for Ferdinand and Miranda. It is also used by Ariel to send the Neapolitans to sleep, and discordant music accompanies the plotting of Sebastian and Alonso. Stephano and Trinculo dance to music to celebrate finding each other. We also hear music for the harpies scene, and on 'Marvellous sweet music' music seems to come from the air. *Prospero's Books* pits words against images and supplements this with sound effects as often as with music; indeed, Michael Nyman's score can in some ways be seen as essentially

6 Michael Anderegg, *Cinematic Shakespeare* (Lanham, MD: Rowman & Littlefield, 2004), p. 193.

just another sound effect.[7] An exception is Mazursky's *Tempest*, of which Douglas Bruster comments that 'The film is full of dancing and dance music'.[8] The *Silent Shakespeare* version of Stow's *The Tempest* also has music by Laura Rossi, whose score heightens atmosphere and creates *leitmotiven*. Violin and piano alternate with guitar, which is used as a motif for Ferdinand (at one point the guitar is playing a recognisably Spanish tune, presumably in a nod to his Spanish descent). The piano strikes up again when he and Miranda are shifting logs together, his instrument mingling with hers in a sign of their coupledom. Though this is a modern addition to the film, screenings of it would originally have been accompanied by live music which might well have worked in much the same ways.

In Jarman, there is breathing rather than title music at the beginning and silence over the closing credits. Fairground music plays at one point, but many scenes have no soundtrack except the dialogue or occasional sounds of wind and wave (the closing credits list this as 'Electronic sound and music by Wavemaker'); we hear music by Gheorghe Zamfir and his orchestra for the dance, but for the most part this is an isle which is *not* full of noises. The 'Marvellous sweet music' is notably raucous and rowdy. Musical effects are reserved primarily for the grand finale, when Elisabeth Welch sings *Stormy Weather*, and are used there with primarily ironic intent: William Pencak notes that Jarman 'considered "stormy

[7] For an analysis of the ways in which Nyman's score supports the cinematography and 'helps the audience find narrative and emotional bearings', see Elsie Walker, 'The Aesthetic Construction of Musical Forms in *Prospero's Books*', in *Peter Greenaway's Prospero's Books: Critical Essays*, edited by Christel Stalpaert (Ghent: Academia Press, 2000), pp. 161–179, p. 162.

[8] Douglas Bruster, 'The Postmodern Theater of Paul Mazursky's *Tempest*', in *Shakespeare, Film, Fin-de-Siècle*, edited by Mark Thornton Burnett and Ramona Wray (Basingstoke: Macmillan, 2000), pp. 26–39, p. 30.

weather" a real possibility following Miranda and Ferdinand's wedding',[9] since, as Steven Dillon observes, 'the marriage that Jarman's *The Tempest* celebrates is the creative relationship between Ariel and Prospero, not the forthcoming marriage of Miranda and Ferdinand';[10] indeed Rowland Wymer cites Toyah Wilcox's 'claim that, when watching the dancing sailors, she was trying to convey through her expression the thought, "These are all good looking men (,) what am I doing with this creep!'.[11]

Most centrally, the whole question of the order of events in The Tempest poses an obvious problem for film. Received Hollywood wisdom is that the hero should face a choice or crisis within the first 20 minutes of the narrative, or the audience's attention will wander. Prospero is faced with such a crisis 12 years before the events of the play begin, and experiences another, smaller-scale one towards the end of Act V: nothing could be more uncongenial to the preferred shape of filmic narrative. Different adaptations adopt different solutions to this problem, none of which is entirely without its attendant difficulties. In Bender's *Tempest*, it is not until scene vi/ 30 minutes in that we see the conjuring of the storm, which has to be on dry land (though Antonio and his companions are in a rowing boat at the time: everything until then has been showing us what happened before the point at which the play opens). In Stow's film, the first four scenes are devoted to backstory; however, this has strongly negative effects, as Judith Buchanan observes: 'whereas the processes and effects of *remembering* the past are

[9] William Pencak, *The Films of Derek Jarman* (Jefferson, NC: McFarland & Co, 2002), pp. 100–1, 102, 106 and 100.
[10] Dillon, *Derek Jarman and Lyric Film*, p. 96.
[11] Rowland Wymer, *Derek Jarman* (Manchester: Manchester University Press, 2005), p. 79.

one of the driving impetuses of the play, the film removes the disrupting function of memory from the drama by ironing out the play's eloquent a-chronologies'.[12] Paul Mazursky's 1982 version uses lengthy flashbacks to tell the backstory, and the storm comes at the end. In *The Animated Tales*, the combination of time constraints and the use of a narrator shrinks the backstory down, while in *Prospero's Books* it is suggested rather than told, in a series of rather fragmented images. In *Forbidden Planet*, the problem is inevitably rather different: a rapid initial summary supplemented by a later account from Morbius suffices admirably, because part of the point is that we are not actually sure what happened and suspect Morbius's version of events to be partial and unreliable. Perhaps most interesting is Jarman's solution, where the backstory is split into two: first Miranda speaks of the women who tended her, then much later, in scene vii (33 minutes in), Prospero gives the 'Twelve years since' speech. (Very oddly, though, Miranda can already name his brother as Antonio.) Moreover, the fact that Prospero is asleep at the start of the film confuses the reality of events in a way rather similar to *Forbidden Planet*. The clear pathologising of Prospero here makes us inevitably less interested in what has happened to him in the past than in what he may do in the future, and so minimises the dangers of beginning in *medias res*.

It is less predictable that so many of the film adaptations should struggle with the concept of an island setting: *Forbidden Planet*, Bender, Jarman, and the BBC version all in their different ways disregard or subvert the play's idea of an island. *Prospero's Books* may pay lip-service to it in the various associated publications, but its real interest is in buildings. Judith Buchanan observes that 'It is perhaps noticeable that only one of these film-makers – Mazursky

---

[12] Buchanan, *Shakespeare on Film*, p. 27.

– has chosen to try to represent the requisite anxiety-provoking space by locating the drama on an actual island, and doing so only succeeded in rendering banal the play's excitingly peripheral zones of mythic and imaginative extravagance'.[13] Perhaps by the same token, adaptations have generally proved equally unwilling to admit the isolation which Shakespeare's play shows even amongst the small group of characters on the island. In the play, Miranda shows no awareness of Ariel's existence, but in adaptation after adaptation a bond is clearly shown between the two – as in *Forbidden Planet*, where Robby makes Alta's clothes; in Bender's version and Mazursky's *Tempest*, where Miranda talks to Ariel rather than her father; and in Jarman's version where Miranda and Ariel are seen together. *Prospero's Books* is the only film that does not suggest such a bond, and here there are so many other people on the island that there is no question of isolation.

It may also seem surprising that so many of these adaptations should tread so carefully around the issue of the relationship between Prospero and Caliban, of which Judith Buchanan comments that

In the Shakespeare play, Prospero's sense of dispossession at having been robbed of his dukedom is mirrored in Caliban's parallel sense of dispossession from *his* kingdom. Equally, Prospero's bitter eloquence about the crimes of the man who has usurped him finds a distorted echo in Caliban's complaint at the unfair treatment he has received at the hands of *his* usurper. And Prospero's consequent desire to punish those who have wronged him finds its cruder equivalent in Caliban's desire for bloody retribution on the man he feels has wronged *him*. The

[13] Buchanan, *Shakespeare on Film*, p. 178.

discernible parallel in situation and attitude between Prospero and Caliban is, needless to say, not one that Prospero himself is eager to own.[14]

However, in every adaptation here discussed, the line 'This thing of darkness I acknowledge mine' falls flat; indeed in Jarman's it does not even appear. Kenneth Branagh's *Hamlet* posits an uncanny connection between Branagh's Hamlet and his ostensible opposite, Derek Jacobi's Claudius; but no film of *The Tempest* countenances any such Gothicising link between two apparently polar opposites.

Instead, every possible strategy is employed to put distance between Prospero and Caliban. Even *Forbidden Planet*, which may seem to be the obvious exception, sharply differentiates between the two in the sequence where Dr Morbius dissociates himself from the actions of his id and effectively separates himself from it. No other adaptation even comes close to suggesting a connection between the two, apart from Mazursky's *Tempest*, in which Phillip acknowledges to Raul Julia's Kalibanos that 'I'm not a god; I'm a monkey just like you' and has earlier said to Kalibanos 'Don't call me boss'. Kalibanos also tells him plainly that Miranda has to sleep with one of them, suggesting an equality which has indeed been implicit since their first meeting, when they introduce themselves to each other with 'I am Kalibanos'; 'I'm Phillip'. Most notably, Phillip asks forgiveness of Kalibanos as well as offering it – although even there, as Douglas Bruster points out, 'Throughout *Tempest*, both story and characters work to show Phillip's impor-tance'.[15] In Bender's film, the difference is one of class; in *The*

[14] Buchanan, *Shakespeare on Film*, p. 154.

[15] Bruster, 'The Postmodern Theater of Paul Mazursky's *Tempest*', p. 34.

Animated Tales, it is virtually one of species; in Stow, in a classic differentiating technique, Prospero has white hair and beard and Caliban, dark. In *Prospero's Books*, Caliban is a creature of the body while Prospero is a man of words; although Prospero and Caliban do appear on screen together, as Deborah Cartmell notes, 'Prospero keeps his distance from Caliban throughout, and there is no physical abuse, let alone contact between the two – in fact, Gielgud remarked that they never actually met during the filming'.[16] In Jarman, the idea occasionally touted that Caliban might even be Prospero's son is dealt a fatal blow by the fact that Caliban is, very unusually, older than Prospero.

Connected to these films' disinclination to acknowledge any bond between Prospero and Caliban is their recurrent preference for a narrator, and their insistent desire to associate that narrator with the Prospero figure. Bender, *Prospero's Books*, *The Animated Tales* and Stow all employ this device, while Mazursky's *Tempest* has occasional captions which gesture in the same direction. In Bender, the first thing we hear is 'My name is Gideon Prosper and this is the story of my life, or rather that part of my life which seems to me to be important'. In one way, this ties in neatly with the great tradition of a questing authorial voice in American fiction, from Melville and Hawthorne on; however, it also serves less radical ends by instantiating Prospero as the undoubted centre of the narrative, with all the other characters just supporting actors. In both Stow and *The Animated Tales*, the narrator is used to give an explicitly or implicitly Christian tone to the story, putting forth a theological schema in which it is easy to read Prospero as right and Caliban as wrong. Moreover, the narration in the *Animated Tales* clearly

[16] Deborah Cartmell, Interpreting *Shakespeare on Screen* (Basingstoke: Macmillan, 2000), p. 83.

directs our sympathies, speaking of 'His wicked brother, Antonio; Alonso, the greedy king of Naples, and *his* treacherous brother, Sebastian' and stressing Alonso's line to Prospero, 'I long to hear the story of your life'. The effect is even more striking in *Prospero's Books*, where Prospero in effect *is* the narrator, or at least certainly supplies a dominant perspective. Again, it is only *Forbidden Planet* and Jarman's film which open up possibilities for interpretation rather than closing them off, by balancing different perspectives against each other rather than allowing one to overwhelm the others.

Film adaptations have also shown uncertainty about *The Tempest*'s genre. The *Animated Tales* version is one of only two directed by Stanislav Sokolov, the other being *The Winter's Tale,* so the two seem to be grouped together as Last Plays. Mazursky's Tempest has several comic elements: Kalibanos is definitely comic; Miranda's borrowing of the phrase 'folie à deux' from Aretha follows a classic gag structure, as does the fact that the boat, for Kalibanos, goes from carrying 100 tourists to 200 to 1000, like Falstaff's 11 men in buckram; and there is a happy ending, with Prospero and Antonia getting back together and Aretha and Alonso seeming mutually attracted. However, although the story ends with kisses all round, the groups are in different spaces; when Phillip gets them to build a theatre, Aretha wants to know if it's for a Euripides play rather than suggesting an Aristophanes one. It is perhaps suggestive that the final sequence is of arrival in Manhattan and we then cut to goats, since the root of the Greek word for tragedy is usually identified as 'goatsong'.

Jarman's *The Tempest* has several elements that are at least potentially tragic, yet Rowland Wymer argues that 'The interlude of dancing sailors ... is the first scene in the film to be fully lit and its evocation of Gilbert and Sullivan operas and Hollywood musicals is a playful breach of generic decorum which temporarily throws off the weight of the world and all its expectations'.[17] Bender's version can perhaps best be classified as pseudo-history with an overlay of magic; Stow's is primarily comic in its affinities; *Prospero's Books* can to some extent be seen as attempting to find a modern equivalent for the masque; while *Forbidden Planet* is pure sci-fi, although Robert F. Willson argues that 'In *Forbidden Planet* the implausible events and characters recall the main figures of Shakespeare's *The Tempest*, grounding the film in a tragicomic context'.[18] *The Animated Tales* version is fantasy. No two of these films could be said to strike the same generic note.

One thing in which these adaptations do largely concur, how-ever, is in not finding Miranda a particularly interesting character. Greenaway typically has her asleep or silent. Jarman challenged conservatives by his casting of his Miranda, but Toyah Wilcox's actual performance falls rather flat – largely because, as she herself admitted, she struggled to make sense of the lines she had to speak. Mazursky's Miranda is a naïve and not particularly interesting teenager: she says of herself, 'I'm not exactly beautiful. Besides I'm a virgin', and when Freddy kisses her she produces the brilliantly deflating line, 'I'm not on the pill so I guess that's all there is'. In both the Stow and the *Animated Tales* versions, Miranda's sole function is to look pretty. The only screen Miranda who is really developed as a character in her own right is Anne Francis's Altairs, who plays a prominent part throughout the film and is allowed to develop attributes and characteristics well beyond those in the rather sketchily sourced character. Moreover, even if the main one

[17] Wymer, *Derek Jarman*, p. 79.

[18] Robert F. Willson, Jr, *Shakespeare in Hollywood, 1929–1956* (London: Associated University Presses, 2000), p. 107.

of these is her flirtatiousness, she does make an independent moral decision when she chooses Adams over Morbius.

Another general point of agreement is that on the screen, in marked contrast to what has happened on the stage, Caliban is never black. For Greenaway, he is a dancer; for Jack Bender, he is white trash; for Jarman, he is a blind man with a Northern accent; for the BBC version, he is lumpen and hairy; for Mazursky, he is Greek; for the *Animated Tales,* he is deformed; and for Stow, he is a wild man. But for all of them, he is white. Only in *Forbidden Planet* is he not specifically marked as such, but it is presumably implicit in the fact that he represents Prospero's id. This is ultimately because all of the films, even Jarman's – which, while it is not hetero-normative, is conservative in other ways – are invested in traditional hegemonies. It also serves to mark the extent of the divide between academic understandings of the play and the image of it presented on film. Although literary criticism may not have all the answers, this is one area in which it has at least attempted to bring an informed political awareness to the play.

The Tempest, then, proves to be a film which is in many ways readily amenable to adaptation, and yet has never spawned any one adaptation that has been universally acclaimed (though *Prospero's Books* and Jarman's version both have their admirers and have generated a good deal of analysis). My own vote for the most interesting and engaging adaptation would go to *Forbidden Planet*, which I think cuts straight to the heart of much of what *The Tempest* meant in its own day, at the same time as showing at least some of what it can mean to ours. But then, it could be argued that it is not in fact an adaptation of *The Tempest* at all. Despite many attempts, a definitive version of *The Tempest* still lies in the future.

PART 3:

Critical responses and the afterlife of text and film

introduction

∙∙

In her book *Shakespeare on Film*, Judith Buchanan declares that 'Appropriately in relation to material deriving from such a fantastical source, the small clutch of film adaptations that have emerged are all quirky or idiosyncratic in some way. As are their makers'.[1] Tony Howard is even more dismissive of those who have attempted screen adaptations of the play when he writes that '*The Tempest*'s allure for ageing male directors is obvious'.[2] (No version that I know of has been directed by a woman.) However, in '"Knowing I Lov'd My Books": Shakespeare, Greenaway, and the Prosperous Dialectics of Word and Image', Claus Schatz-Jacobsen refers to 'the number of more or less felicitous cinematic adaptations to which *The Tempest* has been subjected over the years'.[3] The fact that any adaptation of *The Tempest* could be thought

 [1] Judith Buchanan, *Shakespeare on Film* (Longman: Pearson, 2005), p. 150.

[2] Tony Howard, 'Shakespeare's Cinematic Offshoots', in *The Cambridge Companion to Shakespeare on Film*, edited by Russell Jackson (Cambridge: Cambridge University Press, 2000), pp. 295–313, p. 307.

[3] Claus Schatz-Jacobsen, '"Knowing I Lov'd My Books": Shakespeare, Greenaway, and the Prosperous Dialectics of Word and Image', in *Screen Shakespeare*, edited by Michael Skovmand (Aarhus: Aarhus University Press, 1994), pp. 132–147, p. 132.

felicitous may perhaps seem surprising, given Anthony Miller's contention that

> Though its supernatural spectacles might seem to suit it to the magical technologies of cinema, *The Tempest* has tended to resist direct translation to film. This resistance may derive from other features of the text. The play's large-scale spectacle is balanced by the small-scale intimacy of many of its scenes, which gives it a character akin to chamber music. Shakespeare's observance of the theatrical unities generates a rather small number of rather long scenes ... All these features suit the text to the live theatre rather than the cinema.

However Miller himself concedes that

> One pleasure the films offer is the recognition of ... original Shakespearean features in their modern cinematic guise. This activity of recognition affords the modern audience its equivalent to the Renaissance pleasure in 'imitation,' the reimagining of classical texts in a Renaissance guise.[4]

There has certainly been a vigorous, if not always entirely favourable, critical response to several of the films discussed in this book, even if many of the critics who have come from a background in film studies have struggled a bit when it comes to relating adaptations of *The Tempest* to the original text – as when Steven Dillon misquotes Prospero as calling Ariel 'my trixie spirit',[5] or when

[4] Anthony Miller, '"In this last tempest": Modernising Shakespeare's *Tempest* on Film', *Sydney Studies in English* 23 (1997), pp. 24-40, pp. 24 and 25.

[5] Steven Dillon, *Derek Jarman and Lyric Film* (Texas: University of Texas Press, 2004), p. 96.

William Pencak thinks that *The Tempest* was originally performed at Stoneleigh Abbey.[6] In general, though, the critical debate on these films has been lively and informative. I will discuss first the response to Jarman, then that to Greenaway, and finally that to *Forbidden Planet*.

[6] William Pencak, *The Films of Derek Jarman* (Jefferson, NC: McFarland & Co, 2002), pp. 100–1, 102, 106 and 100.

jarman's *the tempest*

In *Shakespeare's Caliban: A Cultural History*, Alden T. Vaughan and Virginia Mason Vaughan are generally dismissive of adaptations of *The Tempest*:

> Though it has been presented repeatedly on film throughout the twentieth century, no director of Olivier's or Branagh's stature has attempted a popular cinematic version. Instead, *Tempest* films are roughly divided between low-budget television presentations and more expensive adaptations that abandon Shakespeare's text altogether.[7]

They hope, rather forlornly, that 'someday a director of stature and popular appeal – Kenneth Branagh, perhaps – will film Shakespeare's *Tempest* with imagination and technical innovation as well as fidelity to the text. As perhaps the dramatist's most spectacular play, *The Tempest* is ripe for film's fluidity of visual image'.[8]

[7] Alden T. Vaughan and Virginia Mason Vaughan, *Shakespeare's Caliban: A Cultural History* (Cambridge: Cambridge University Press, 1991), p. 200.
[8] Vaughan and Vaughan, *Shakespeare's Caliban*, p. 214.

The Vaughans were writing before *Prospero's Books* was released,[9] when Jarman's *The Tempest* was the only arthouse offering. However, they clearly do not rate Jarman's film, and this is not surprising: Jarman himself, in the interview included in 'Special Features' of the DVD of his *Tempest*, remarks on its lack of popularity with Americans. As Sara Martin notes,

Cinema audiences in Britain responded well to Jarman's challenge – at least the small audience that felt addressed by Jarman's film. *The Tempest* was originally released at the Edinburgh Film Festival to high acclaim, but flopped in the US. A furious attack mounted by Vincent Canby, the *New York Times* critic, destroyed not only the film's chances in America but also Jarman's chances to get funding for new projects in the midst of his most fruitful years.[10]

Certainly the Vaughans' distaste for the Jarman film is palpable:

Jarman used Shakespeare's text and characters, so technically his film was not an adaptation. But he transposed so many

[9] In their subsequent Arden edition of *The Tempest*, the Vaughans were reticent about that too – saying merely that it contained 'The most flamboyant twentieth-century representation of Prospero ... in a vehicle screened all over the world, he could, like Bottom, play all the parts' (William Shakespeare, *The Tempest*, edited by Virginia Mason Vaughan and Alden T. Vaughan [London: Thomas Nelson, 2003], introduction, p. 119).

[10] Sara Martin, 'Classic Shakespeare for All: *Forbidden Planet* and *Prospero's Books*, Two Screen Adaptations of *The Tempest*', in *Classics in Film and Fiction*, edited by Deborah Cartmell, I. Q. Hunter, Heidi Kaye and Imelda Whelehan (London: Pluto, 2000), pp. 34–53, p. 37; see also Jarman's own account in *Derek Jarman, Dancing Ledge*, edited by Shaun Allen (London: Quartet Books, 1984), p. 206.

scenes and cut so many lines that the final product seemed little akin to Shakespeare's drama. Rather, it was a remaking of Shakespeare's script into a commentary on the 1970s counter-culture movement.[11]

Equally Kenneth Rothwell calls the Sycorax vignette in Jarman's film 'revolting' and wearily declares that 'Frontal nudity designed to *épater le bourgeois* is a well-worn trope in the films of transgressive cinema' but that actually Jarman's film 'is delivered in decidedly non-transgressive establishment RP accents'.[12]

British critics, however, have generally looked favourably on Jarman's film, though Rowland Wymer cites poor reviews from Frank Kermode and Peter Ackroyd, both of whom thought the verse badly spoken (Kermode exempted Heathcote Williams from this criticism).[13] Even when they are dismissive of certain aspects, British critics tend to be more tolerantly and amusedly so: this thing of darkness they acknowledge theirs, as when John Orr declares that 'Jarman's high camp extravagances often give the viewer the sense of a liberated boy scout troop attempting a nativity play'. For Orr, 'One can speculate that Jarman is high camp because he was also in upbringing High Anglican, because he needed the visual surety of sacred spectacle if only to make it profane'. He is thus typically English (a point often made by critics about Jarman), even though ultimately, judged by that benchmark, he comes up slightly short: 'He aims at times for the eccentric feel of earlier

[11] Vaughan and Vaughan, *Shakespeare's Caliban*, p. 200.

[12] Kenneth S. Rothwell, *A History of Shakespeare on Screen*, 2nd edition (Cambridge: Cambridge University Press, 2004), p. 197.

[13] Rowland Wymer, *Derek Jarman* (Manchester: Manchester University Press, 2005), p. 73.

English film comedy but lacks its formal control. His intellectual concern is really to inflate his subject matter rather than deflate it and for most audiences he draws the sting of tragedy without compensating through humour'.[14]

Other critics have been more willing to concentrate on what Jarman *is,* than on what he is not. David Hawkes claims that

> Jarman's treatment of *The Tempest* (1979) exemplifies his view of the connections between the early modern theatre and the postmodern cinema. By drawing out those aspects of the play – its homoeroticism, its overall concern with sexual dynamics and power relations, and its juxtaposition of narrative with spectacle – which are also pertinent concerns of the cinema, Jarman affirms a kinship between his own work and the early modern theatre, and thus distances the audience from the conventions of narrative cinema.[15]

For Hawkes, Jarman is deploying a sophisticated strategy to make a wide-ranging point: 'By presenting Prospero as an overtly sadistic tyrant, Jarman ... alludes to the connections between the diegetic force driving the narrative forward and sadistic, patriarchal sexuality'.[16] For Rowland Wymer, 'More than anything else, Jarman's *Tempest* is a truly "magical" film which manages to make most

[14] John Orr, 'The Art of National Identity: Peter Greenaway and Derek Jarman', in *British Cinema, Past and Present*, edited by Justine Ashby and Andrew Higson (London: Routledge, 2000), pp. 327–338, pp. 336, 334 and 335.

[15] David Hawkes, '"The shadow of this time": the Renaissance cinema of Derek Jarman', in *By Angels Driven: The Films of Derek Jarman*, edited by Chris Lippard (Trowbridge: Flicks Books, 1996), pp. 103–116, p. 107.

[16] Hawkes, '"The shadow of this time": the Renaissance cinema of Derek Jarman', p. 107.

stage productions look overly literal and leaden-footed and which eludes most of the traps set by academic criticism'; he suggests that for Jarman, 'the play is centrally about childhood, the loss of child-hood, the loss of the imagination, and the approach of death rather than about any positive psychological growth or adaptation'.[17]

Some critics have pointed to the film's sophisticated sense of historical process. William Pencak observes that 'Jarman planned to costume Prospero like Robespierre', while

> The remaining characters embody three centuries of history. Miranda and Ferdinand belong to the ancient regime ... The comedians and Caliban are nineteenth century workers (Caliban is also an exploited colonial), Ariel and the sailors twentieth century minions of the elite.[18]

As Jim Ellis observes,

> The period film's approach to the past can be contrasted with *The Tempest's* costumes, which Jarman says "are a chronology of the 350 years of the play's existence, like the patina on old bronze." They range from what the designer Yolanda Sonnabend describes as Miranda's "heady Hollywood four-teenth century" ball gown to Ariel's overalls and white gloves.

For Ellis, 'Jarman's interest in forgiveness means that the film articulates a possible version of the nation, a happier future, while remembering its unhappy present. It does this primarily by inter-vening in the production of its past'. In particular, he observes that

---

[17] Wymer, *Derek Jarman*, pp. 76 and 78.

[18] Pencak, *The Films of Derek Jarman*, p. 101.

'The masque form ... is crucial to Jarman's project ... His aim, as with the early modern masque, is to create through spectacle the grounds for a new community' because 'By including the conspirators, wearing drag and now included in the final vision of community, the film reverses the masque's historical role in representing the white European body as the incarnation of order'.[19]

A number of critics have engaged with Jarman's representation of homosexuality. Judith Buchanan sees the whole film as structured around Prospero's subconscious coming to terms with his homosexual side. Arguing that 'Initially, Caliban is the only sexually suggestive and overtly camp influence on the island. Gradually, however, he has a widening circle of influence', she suggests that 'Prospero's dream becomes increasingly saturated in gay images as the plot continues to elude his firm control ... his hostility to the Caliban influence in his own mindworld has abated'. For Buchanan, 'Whereas the entertainment scripted by Shakespeare's Prospero formally validates chastity and by promoting sexual deferral, in the sailors' dance Jarman's Prospero licenses a dionysian celebration of sexuality'; she suggests that 'At the opening of the film his sleep had been very troubled: at its close he sleeps peacefully'.[20] However, Deborah Cartmell sees the exact opposite, arguing that 'If Jarman's own homosexuality was not so well known, this could be interpreted as an anti-gay production'.[21]

Kate Chedgzoy also focuses on the film's representation of sexuality, suggesting that 'Jarman's primary interest lies not in

[19] Jim Ellis, 'Conjuring *The Tempest*: Derek Jarman and the Spectacle of Redemption', GLQ 7.2 (2001), pp. 265–84, pp. 267, 265–6, and 278.

[20] Buchanan, *Shakespeare on Film*, pp. 165–7.

[21] Deborah Cartmell, *Interpreting Shakespeare on Screen* (Basingstoke: Macmillan, 2000), p. 80.

proving that Shakespeare was homosexual, but in re-creating, within the terms of his own aesthetic, a range of texts drawn from an international homosexual "great tradition" which includes Caravaggio, Marlowe and Britten as well as Shakespeare'.[22] Chedgzoy is, however, worried by some of the ideological implications of Jarman's film: 'Arguably, the highly pleasurable experience of watching the film uses cinematic magic to reconcile the viewer to the dispositions made by Prospero'; 'Jarman's depiction of Sycorax does nothing to query the misogyny and racism of Shakespeare's text in this respect'.[23] Colin MacCabe also engages with this issue:

> It is fashionable at the moment, in the current jargon of post-coloniality, to read *The Tempest* entirely in relation to Caliban ... From this point of view Jarman's *Tempest* is an embarassment, for his Caliban is white and the concerns of colonialism are largely absent from his film. But these contemporary readings ignore another, and as important, political reading which concentrates on the formation of the new nation-states which will dominate global history for the next four centuries. Explicitly, these concerns are present in *The Tempest* in terms of the politics of the court of Milan. Jarman rigorously excludes all such concerns from his film.

The last sentence may come as something of a surprise, given the direction MacCabe's argument is apparently taking, but he does go on to offer a more recuperative reading when he claims that 'In *The Tempest*, however, (Jarman) makes clear how Prospero's

[22] Kate Chedgzoy, *Shakespeare's Queer Children: Sexual Politics and Contemporary Culture* (Manchester: Manchester University Press, 1995), p. 182.
[23] Chedgzoy, *Shakespeare's Queer Children*, pp. 200 and 204.

reign is one of terror'. MacCabe sees this as a deliberate rebuff to the Tillyard school, which saw 'the Elizabethan age as one of social harmony'. For MacCabe,

> The crucial element in this machinery of terror was Walsingham's secret service, and we can read Ariel in *The Tempest* as an allegory of that secret service, forced under pitiless conditions to spy on every corner of the island and to bring his master Prospero that information which underpins his power. It is for this reason that Jarman's *Tempest* concentrates on the relationship between Prospero and Ariel with its barely suppressed sexual undertones. Jarman's homosexuality is what leads him to concentrate on the repression at the heart of the English state from which all the other repressions follow.[24]

MacCabe feels, however, that *The Tempest* is only partially successful in this, and that it is not until *Edward II* that Jarman fully articulates his vision of the way in which the modern state works, and how the Elizabethan state helps us to understand this.

Jim Ellis finds a more radical reading of *The Tempest*. He argues that '"the concerns of colonialism" are not in fact absent from the film, in spite of Caliban's and Sycorax's apparent whiteness', and suggests that

> A black Caliban is ... an invitation to unwitting anachronisms, and although these anachronisms may well prove productive,

24 Colin MacCabe, 'A Post-National European Cinema: A Consideration of Derek Jarman's *The Tempest* and *Edward II*', in *Shakespeare on Film: Contemporary Critical Essays*, edited by Robert Shaughnessy (Basingstoke: Palgrave, 1998), pp. 145–155, pp. 148–9.

we might consider whether there are other ways of playing Caliban's otherness that could unveil in less expected ways the origins and dimensions of British racialist thinking.

By contrast,

Might portraying Caliban as an appetitive, physically excessive, working-class Northerner remind us that "most tropes of black-ness operate within a larger discursive network" and that race, moreover, has very little to do with the slight biological difference that naturalizes a whole array of cultural codings? Is Caliban, in this version, still functioning as a racial other?

Ellis further argues that

In spite of the author's biological whiteness, Sycorax's geo-graphic origins are not completely effaced. Rather than being signaled by skin tone, however, they are signified by European signs of oriental depravity, right down to the hookah Sycorax smokes.

He contends that

... by making Sycorax white but North African, physically "disordered" and moreover sexually threatening, the film foregrounds the interconnections of racism and misogyny in colonialist discourse and the means by which this discourse constructed racial otherness, without at the same time reforging these links in the film's visual economy.

For Ellis, this is merely one of the film's transgressive and subversive discourses, another being provided by its choice of music for the final scene:

> The blues, like camp or alchemy, is a marginal discourse invested in transformation, one that displays faith in the transformational power of art. The history of the blues is of course bound up with the history of slavery, racism, and colonialism ... We might also note that "Stormy Weather" has a significant performance history, associated primarily with black divas.

Ultimately, then, he argues that 'The combination of camp and blues in the final scene combines the two communities continually read as threats to British nationhood in the postwar era, queers and blacks'.[25] William Pencak similarly reads Jarman's Caliban as African on the grounds that the one in the play is, and argues that 'Miranda, at least at first, seems torn between her pseudo-Afro dreadlock hairstyle (representing nature and suggesting some affinity for Caliban) and her dress, standing for civilization, which is in tatters from the beginning'.[26]

[25] Ellis, 'Conjuring *The Tempest*', pp. 267–70 and 278–9.
[26] Pencak, *The Films of Derek Jarman*, pp. 103–4.

prospero's books

••

Response to Greenaway's film has been mixed. Graham Holderness and Christopher McCullough's 'Shakespeare on the Screen: A Selective Filmography', in *Shakespeare and the Moving Image*, excludes *Prospero's Books* altogether; in the book's index it is labelled 'Adaptation'. In his essay in the volume, Russell Jackson remarks that 'Greenaway's film sometimes seems like a deluxe version of Jarman's (both show us Sycorax, for example), but its refusal to tell the play's story simply is its undoing as anything other than the "adaptation" it claims to be'. Jackson says of *Prospero's Books* that 'it illustrates the story rather than playing it out'.[27] Amy Lawrence comments that 'The literary descriptions of Prospero's books find Greenaway caught between the written and the cinematic. Many of his descriptions contain things that cannot be visualized'.[28] H. R. Coursen is entirely dismissive, complaining of the

[27] Russell Jackson, 'Shakespeare's Comedies on Film', in *Shakespeare and the Moving Image: The Plays on Film and Television*, edited by Anthony Davies and Stanley Wells (Cambridge: Cambridge University Press, 1994), pp. 99–120, pp. 109 and 110.

[28] Lawrence, *The Films of Peter Greenaway*, p. 152.

film's use of allusions that 'we are not *learning* anything. Our ignorance is being exposed, no doubt, but that darkness is not being lightened by Greenaway's display of what *he* knows',[29] and Chantal Zabus and Kevin A Dwyer dismissively declare that 'Greenaway's main concern is with sources and origins, fossilizing *The Tempest*-as-Bardscript in the cloven pine of the baroque, with an excess of ornaments and repetitive allusions'. They add,

> Greenaway's film is clearly bulimic because of the general philosophy of display, the cultivation *ad libidum* of the huge masque or fresco, because of the sheer surplus or cornucopia of allusions that obscure the ultimate goal of the film, but also because of the excessive extra-cinematic information that Greenaway provides in interviews.

For Zabus and Dwyer, 'Greenaway spends a lot of time congratulating and explaining himself, most of the time taking his hat off to European high culture during the Renaissance, which he considers a period of pure Enlightenment. Greenaway also takes care to mention only European rewritings of *The Tempest* ... but none of the post-colonial ones'.[30] Even the generally positive Eckart Voigts-Virchow sounds a note of ambivalence in his conclusion that 'Greenaway changes the way we see: *Prospero's Books*', see-changes turn cinema into something richer, stranger, more self-

[29] H. R. Coursen, *Watching Shakespeare on Television* (London and Toronto: Associated University Presses, 1993), p. 166.

[30] Chantal Zabus and Kevin A. Dwyer, '"I'll be wise hereafter": Caliban in Postmodern British Cinema', in *Constellation Caliban: Figurations of a Character*, edited by Nadia Lie and Theo D'haen (Amsterdam: Rodopi, 1997), pp. 271–289, pp. 281, 282 and 285.

indulgent',[31] while Michael Anderegg grudgingly concedes that 'Like the Caliban of the film, as Douglas Lanier suggests, Greenaway is a desecrater of books who nevertheless saves them from oblivion'.[32]

However, Herbert Klein quite simply declares that '*Prospero's Books* is an ideal portrayal of cognitive and pragmatic change'. For him,

> Prospero is not merely the protagonist of the play, but also its creator. The play is a product of his mind and a result of his own imagination. The main level with the film versions of theatre plays i.e. the addition of another level of communication by the narrating cinema is, on the one hand, doubly intensified by the narrator's dual identity, yet on the other hand, the problem is solved because presentation and narrative are united.[33]

Similarly, Dan DeWeese observes that 'If there is a director suited to the "ethos" (to use Bloom's term) of late Shakespeare, it is probably Greenaway. Shakespeare, after all, was not averse to a good, self-referential joke ... and neither did he refrain from calling attention to the constructed nature of his plays'. DeWeese notes that 'One could go through the entire film watching only the deep background and find more than enough visual material to keep the eye busy; even in shadows that appear to be a hundred yards

[31] Voigts-Virchow, 'Something richer, stranger, more self-indulgent', p. 95.
[32] Michael Anderegg, *Cinematic Shakespeare* (Lanham, MD: Rowman & Littlefield, 2004), p. 200.
[33] Herbert Klein, '"The far side of the mirror": Peter Greenaway's *Prospero's Books*', *Erfurt Electronic Studies in English* (1996).
Online: http://webdoc.sub.gwdg.de/edoc/ia/eese/eese.html

from the camera, there are often barely-visible figures lurking'.[34] As if to exemplify this, Mariacristina Cavecchi announces that 'My analysis will be limited to the exploration of the spatial field ... created by Greenaway in the first sequences of the shipwreck',[35] while Kenneth Rothwell observes that '*Prospero's Books* contains the ingredients for three doctoral dissertations in film studies'. Rothwell concludes that even though it is 'notably humorless, (and) the movie leaves you intellectually gorged but emotionally starved', 'there is a numinous sense of being in the presence of a masterpiece that makes glib dismissals egregiously philistine'.[36]

Many critics have indeed seen great artistry in *Prospero's Books*. Mariacristina Cavecchi argues that 'In the decision to create an outdoor effect indoors, the filmmaker follows Shakespeare's mounting a storm complete with a shipwreck on an indoor stage'. For her, 'the image of the model galleon ... is also a hint at the special effects of the cinema (since many storm scenes have been shot using model ships)'. She suggests that 'Greenaway uses the frame-within-frame as the cinematic equivalent of Shakespeare's play-within-play', points out that 'repetition is a fundamental recurring stylistic device in *The Tempest*', and ultimately argues that 'The audience is ... established as the subject of the film, occupying a polysemic site where a multiplicity of possible meanings and intertextual relationships intersect'.[37]

[34] Dan DeWeese, 'Prospero's Pharmacy: Peter Greenaway and the Critics Play Shakespeare's Mimetic Game', in *Almost Shakespeare: Reinventing his Works for Cinema and Television*, edited by James R. Keller and Leslie Stratyner (Jefferson, NC: McFarland and Company, 2004), pp. 155–168, pp. 158–9 and 160.

[35] Mariacristina Cavecchi, 'Peter Greenaway's *Prospero's Books*: A Tempest Between Word and Image', *Literature Film Quarterly* 25.2 (1979), pp. 83–9, p. 83.

[36] Rothwell, *A History of Shakespeare on Screen*, pp. 199, 202, and 200.

[37] Cavecchi, 'Peter Greenaway's *Prospero's Books*', pp. 85–87.

Similarly, Judith Buchanan remarks on the suggestiveness of the visual allusion of Prospero's cell to Da Messina's painting of *St Jerome in His Study*,[38] and Peter S Donaldson suggests that 'the repeated shots of Gielgud's writing fingers may allude to the medium of composition through the ambiguity of the word "digital," which can refer to the works of the hand or the effects of computation'.[39]

Developing this line, many critics have commented on the film's use of numbers. Greenaway himself notes Prospero's metaphor of thirds (V.i.312) and comments on the way in which the first third of the film is separate.[40] As Martin Butler notes,

> Nearly half the screenplay – forty-three of its ninety-one scenes – is devoted to Shakespeare's first act, and this Greenaway labels "The Past". The effect is to underline how much *The Tempest*'s action creates Prospero's story as a chain of links, a personal history that he makes or recovers. Greenaway's Prospero is acquiring a virtual subjectivity: his self is, essentially, his power of retrieval.[41]

Sara Martin notes that 'there are 24 books in Prospero's library, the number of frames per second of film',[42] and along similar lines Eckart Voigts-Virchow observes that 'Greenaway furthermore

[38] Buchanan, *Shakespeare on Film*, p. 226.

[39] Peter S. Donaldson, 'Shakespeare in the Age of Post-Mechanical Reproduction: Sexual and electronic magic in *Prospero's Books*', in *Shakespeare, the Movie: Popularizing the plays on film, TV, and video*, edited by Lynda E. Boose and Richard Burt (London: Routledge, 1997), pp. 169–185, p. 171.

[40] Greenaway, *Prospero's Books*, p. 134.

[41] Butler, 'Prospero in Cyberspace', p. 190.

[42] Martin, 'Classic Shakespeare for All', pp. 45–6.

subdivides his film into 91 sections, which correspond to changes in locations (and to the fact that the film was made in 1991?)'. Peggy Phelan declares,

> With Greenaway (as with Shakespeare), numbers are always metaphorical and literal. One hundred in *Prospero's Books* is the always approaching but never fully arrived at moment of completion. On both the micro and macro level the film is structured around coherently symmetrical forms which are constantly imitated and gestured toward but which twist or fail to unify at the last minute.

She notes too that 'Twenty-four is an appealing number for Greenaway. Twenty-four frames makes up one second of film and twenty-four hours makes up one day (*The Tempest* observes the unities, so twenty-four books should make a full and coherent library for a practicing Magus)'.[43] (Twenty-four years was, of course, also the span of life and power for which Faustus bargained in Marlowe's play, which has so often been related to Shakespeare's.)

However, even generally favourable critics can see drawbacks to the film's layered and difficult visual style. Mariacristina Cavecchi observes that 'Greenaway develops and focuses on the aesthetic and mannerist aspects of the Shakespearean text, while he does not seem to care too much about the other very important Shakespearean themes',[44] and Steven Marx comments, 'Peter Greenaway's film, *Prospero's Books*, has developed a small cult following, but most people who try can't sit through it. If you don't

---

[43] Peggy Phelan, 'Numbering Prospero's Books', *Performing Arts Journal* 14.2 (1992), pp. 43–50, p. 45.

[44] Cavecchi, 'Peter Greenaway's *Prospero's Books*', p. 83.

know the book it's based on, Shakespeare's *The Tempest*, the film is likely to make no sense at all'.[45] Jonathan Romney also offers blame as well as praise: 'By presenting too much to take in at a glance, Greenaway tests to the limit his ideal of a painterly cinema'.[46]

Those critics who have attempted to tease out the film's layers of meaning have adopted a variety of approaches. Paula Willoquet-Maricondi sees it as a film that 'express(es) our contemporary concerns with the power of science and technology to alter and destroy the ecosystemic relations on which hinges the survival of all beings', declaring that 'The central role given to Caliban's body in the film serves to suggest an alternative means of playfully experiencing the world and constitutes an antidote to Prospero's hegemonic rationalism'. (She contrasts this with the many head shots of Prospero.)[47] Steven Marx, in 'Progeny: *Prospero's Books*, Genesis and *The Tempest*', argues that the Bible, and particularly the Book of Genesis, is 'a generative template' for the film.[48] Certainly *Prospero's Books* does seem to be interested in the Bible, even though, rather surprisingly for the period, none of Prospero's books *is* a Bible. (Perhaps, as in *Desert Island Discs*,

---

[45] Steven Marx, 'Progeny: *Prospero's Books*, Genesis and *The Tempest*', *Renaissance Forum* 1.2 (September 1996).
Online: http://www.hull.ac.uk/renforum/v1no2/marx.htm

[46] Romney, Review of *Prospero's Books*, p. 145.

[47] Paula Willoquet-Maricondi, 'Aimé Césaire's *A Tempest* and Peter Greenaway's *Prospero's Books* as Ecological Rereadings and Rewritings of Shakespeare's *The Tempest*', in *Reading the Earth: New Directions in the Study of Literature and Environment*, edited by Michael P. Branch, Rochelle Johnson, Daniel Patterson, and Scott Slovic (Moscow, Idaho: University of Idaho Press, 1998), pp. 209–224, pp. 209 and 218.

[48] Marx, 'Progeny: *Prospero's Books*, Genesis and *The Tempest*'.

the Bible and the works of Shakespeare are taken as givens.) Greenaway himself observed that 'in this script it is intended that there should be some deliberate cross-identification between Prospero, Shakespeare and Gielgud. At times they are indivisibly one person', in terms clearly reminiscent of the idea of the Holy Trinity; he also speaks of Prospero's 'crozier-like wand',[49] and there are church bells and candelabras after Prospero promises to renounce magic. In a further article five years later, Marx develops the idea of indebtedness to the Bible and extends it to Revelation as well as Genesis: 'Like those of the Book of Revelation, the literary conventions of *Prospero's Books* and of the whole of *The Tempest* are contained within the genre of masque. Masques are dream visions staged with illusory spectacles so overwhelming they challenge the reality of the waking world'.[50]

This observation in turn leads Marx on to examine the importance of masque motifs in Greenaway's film: 'Masque devices include falling asleep and awakening, moving into or away from framed images and mirrors, opening and closing curtains and doors, and performances that start and break off'.[51] Other critics also comment on this: Sara Martin, for instance, argues that 'Greenaway pays as much homage to Inigo Jones, the celebrated masque designer, as to late twentieth-century technology',[52] while Eckart Voigts-Virchow notes that 'the visual and aural exuberance of *Prospero's Books* turns it into an extended masque, blending

[49] Peter Greenaway, *Prospero's Books: A Film of Shakespeare's* The Tempest (London: Chatto & Windus, 1991), pp. 9 and 162.
[50] Steven Marx, 'Greenaway's Books', *Early Modern Literary Studies* 7.2 (September, 2001). Online: http://www.shu.ac.uk/emls/07-2/marxgree.htm
[51] Marx, 'Greenaway's Books'.
[52] Martin, 'Classic Shakespeare for All', p. 45.

music, dance and scenery into a full exploitation of whatever means the cinema at the end of the 20th century has to offer in recreating a Jones/Jonson-*Gesamtkunstwerk*'.[53] Adam Barker observes of Greenaway that 'His heroes include modernists such as the painter R. B. Kitaj and the composer John Cage, but also Jacobean dramatists such as Ford and Webster. He is especially drawn to the masque form – the courtly entertainment'.[54]

The comparison with Ford in particular is one often made. Greenaway himself declared: 'I have thought often of seeing if a modern Jacobean drama was possible, to shift Webster and Ford to the twentieth century',[55] and Laura Denham compares Greenaway to Ford, though she mistakenly thinks that it is Annabella's head which Giovanni skewers on his dagger rather than her heart – a pity, for if she had read *'Tis Pity She's a Whore* more closely, she would have been able to relate it to both the importance of pregnancy and birth in Greenaway's *oeuvre* and the importance of stomach imagery, particularly in *The Belly of an Architect*, on both of which she also comments.[56]

Peter Donaldson and Martin Butler, by contrast, look at the film not as the resurrection of an old genre, but as the birth of a new one. In Donaldson's analysis, '*Prospero's Books* is an anticipatory or proleptic allegory of the digital future, figuring the destruction of libraries and their rebirth as "magically" enhanced electronic

[53] Voigts-Virchow, 'Something richer, stranger, more self-indulgent', p. 93.

[54] Adam Barker, 'A Tale of Two Magicians', in *Film/Literature/Heritage: A Sight and Sound Reader*, edited by Ginette Vincendeau (London: British Film Institute, 2001), pp. 109–115, p. 112.

[55] Alan Woods, *Being Naked Playing Dead: The Art of Peter Greenaway* (Manchester: Manchester University Press, 1996), p. 239.

[56] Laura Denham, *The Films of Peter Greenaway* (London: Minerva Press, 1993), pp. 30–1; see also pp. 36 and 20.

books',[57] while in Butler's, 'With its proliferating layers of "windows", its sedimentation of imagery and text, and the amazing moving pictures it invents for Prospero's books, the film imitates the conventions of electronic text production that, at the time of its release, were just beginning to impact significantly on everyday life'.[58]

Another insistent concern of critics, as with Jarman, has been to read back in the post-colonial element. This is something which Greenaway himself entirely ignored, as Sara Martin points out:

> Greenaway has Caliban retrieve the last book that Prospero throws away – Shakespeare's *First Folio*. This gesture is read by Paul Washington as Greenaway's failure to protect the coherence of the postcolonial reading of from the director's own challenge to Shakespeare's authority. Actually, Greenaway questions the now popular postcolonial reading by completely ignoring it.[59]

H. R. Coursen, however, takes issue with this, and indeed uses it as one of the main planks of his indictment of Greenaway:

> One can ignore the "discourse on colonialism," but in doing so, Greenaway ignores that version of "intertextuality" whereby zeitgeist can inform a work of art, as opposed to being an alienated opponent to it.[60]

---

[57] Peter Donaldson, 'Digital Archives and Sibylline Fragments: *The Tempest* and the End of Books', *Postmodern Culture* 8.2 (January 1998). Online (subscription only): http://muse.jhu.edu/journals/postmodern_culture/toc/pmc8.2.html

[58] Martin Butler, 'Prospero in Cyberspace', in *Re-constructing the Book: Literary texts in transmission*, edited by Maureen Bell, Shirley Chew, Simon Eliot, Lynette Hunter and James L. W. West III (Aldershot: Ashgate, 2002), pp. 184–196, p. 189.

[59] Martin, 'Classic Shakespeare for All', p. 45.

[60] Coursen, *Watching Shakespeare on Television*, p. 164.

William Babula incisively comments that although 'In the text, Tunis is for Alonso, the king of Naples, a very acceptable groom for his daughter, Claribel', in *Prospero's Books*

... the arranged and apparently consummated marriage of Claribel and the African King Tunis is depicted in the most grotesque fashion. A miserable and sexually abused Claribel is shown with a bloody pudendum while nude white slave girls attend to the obviously polygamous Tunis.[61]

Chantal Zabus and Kevin A. Dwyer declare that 'Jarman's and Greenaway's adaptations are ... a regeneration of Europe into *The Tempest* story. Their cultural conservatism inevitably goes hand in hand with a professed lack of concern for the post-colonial potentialities of the play'. Zabus and Dwyer further note that

Even when describing the African scenes, Greenaway emphasizes the "high culture" aspect of African civilization ... The natives, Greenaway notes, "as befits (Prospero's) European imagination (...) have the look both of classical figures and of John White's American Indians"... who have indeed been classicized to suit European taste, both aesthetic and sexual.

For them, 'That Caliban salvages the books is further evidence of Greenaway's underestimation of Caliban's rebellious potential. This ambiguous rescue-operation makes Caliban a complicit player in the very story that oppresses him'.[62]

[61] William Babula, 'Claribel, Tunis and Greenaway's *Prospero's Books*', *Journal of the Wooden O Symposium* 2001, pp. 19–25, p. 19.

[62] Zabus and Dwyer, '"I'll be wise hereafter"', pp. 272 and 285.

Others are kinder about Greenaway's treatment – or lack of it – of the issue. Sara Martin notes that the director's Caliban is much less demonised than is often the case: 'whereas other actors dance to music, Clark's innovative Caliban dances to Shakespeare's words', and

Greenaway ... invests much more creativity in imagining the monster Caliban than the angelic Ariel. In consonance with the variety of human bodies and the overlapping of images on the screen, Ariel is played by four blond, curly-haired actors, whose ages range from seven to about twenty-five and who represent the sum total of the four elements: air, water, earth, fire.[63]

Indeed, even Chantal Zabus and Kevin A. Dwyer offer a partially recuperative reading when they note of Jarman's Caliban, Stephano and Trinculo that 'The butler, cook and sailor represent lower-class male occupations and, as such, hint at the exploited classes of British society' and argue that

In comparison with his presence on the stage in Shakespeare's original, Jarman shows his endearment for Caliban by giving him quite a considerable amount of screen time. Caliban appears in approximately 25 minutes of this 96 minute-long film and his off-screen laughter is often heard long after he exits or even before he enters a scene. Eight minutes of the 25 either comprise scenes which have been added to Shakespeare's text ... or place Caliban in scenes where he is absent in Shakespeare.[64]

[63] Zabus and Dwyer, "'I'll be wise hereafter'", pp. 272 and 285.
[64] Martin, 'Classic Shakespeare for All', p. 47.

Greenaway is, however, seen by many critics as creating monsters of other kinds. Adam Barker notes that 'Greenaway's films are littered with flawed male protagonists whose arrogance and grandiose artistic schemes are ultimately their undoing', and that his 'work has often been accused of misogyny because of the extreme humiliation suffered by women characters of his films'. Perhaps most strikingly, Barker suggests the film itself as potentially a kind of monster: 'Greenaway is wary of the film being seen as a "technological freak", but believes he has only scratched the surface of the technical possibilities'.[65] Equally Geoffrey Wall characterises the film ambivalently as 'Delirious abundance, like Sainsbury's the week before Christmas ... Is Greenaway's undeclared subtitle perhaps *The Work of Art in the Age of Electronic Reproduction*?'.[66]

Most critics have been more positive about the film's technological advances. Thus Peggy Phelan declares that

All four of Shakespeare's Romances, and especially *The Tempest*, his last, are full of disappearing tricks which seem like embryonic special effects in film. Peter Greenaway's breathtaking cinematic treatment of *The Tempest, Prospero's Books*, accents the strange moment in the history of theatre when drama discovers the beguiling power of visual seduction.

Noting that 'Virtually every frame in *Prospero's Books* operates on at least two planes of space-time', Phelan argues that

Greenaway's lavish use of this technology overthrows the confining rules of perspective which have defined Hollywood film

[65] Barker, 'A Tale of Two Magicians', pp. 113, 114, and 111.
[66] Wall, 'Greenaway Filming *The Tempest*', p. 335.

practice since its inception. The frame is no longer a two-dimensional object. Like a paper model of a cube folded into a book, the frame unfolds and reveals multiple layers of spatial dimensions. The use of perspective in Renaissance painting and theatre set design transformed the spatial dimensions of the square canvas and the flat set: Greenaway's paintbox similarly indicates a radical new way of seeing cinematic space.[67]

Hence, although the film was shot in a disused aircraft hangar in Amsterdam,[68] *Prospero's Books* can be perceived as based in the universal: for Jonathan Romney, for instance, 'Greenaway interprets *The Tempest* as the story of a mind reviewing its entire contents',[69] and the personal dimension is further eroded by the fact that, as Geoffrey Wall notes, Greenaway 'spurns the familiar narrative syntax of Hollywood cinema: the expressive close-up of the human face, the rhythms of shot-reverse-shot synchronised with dialogue. He relishes long travelling shots with deep perspectives framed by mirrors and archways, multiple images that divide the screen, complicated montage sequences'.[70]

Finally, other approaches have also been taken. Despite Greenaway's own reticence on this subject, some critics have attempted to read the film in the light of his biography. Laura Denham notes that after leaving school, Greenaway was employed by the Central Office of Information: 'Greenaway spent the next ten years as an editor in the Government's Crown Film Unit, cutting films that supposedly portrayed the English way of life

[67] Phelan, 'Numbering Prospero's Books', pp. 43 and 44.

[68] Denham, *The Films of Peter Greenaway*, p. 45.

[69] Romney, Review of *Prospero's Books*, p. 143.

[70] Wall, 'Greenaway Filming *The Tempest*', p. 336.

through numbers and statistics'[71] M, E. Warlick, by contrast, argues for the importance of 'an alchemical interpretation' of the film,[72] while H. R. Coursen focuses on a possible influence, referring to 'Prospero's mildly Tolkienesque imagination'[73] – something which is hardly surprising since, as Eckart Voigts-Virchow notes, 'Peter Greenaway confesses his "enthusiasm for J. R. R. Tolkien's *Lord of the Rings*"'. Indeed, for Voigts-Virchow this offers an important key to the film, since 'So far, discussions of Greenaway have failed to see his postmodernist film-making as transformations of the fantastic. Especially *Prospero's Books* (1991), his adaptation of Shakespeare's *The Tempest*, calls for a re-evaulation of elements of the postmodern fantastic in his work'.[74] The range of critical positions and perspectives which critics have brought to bear on Greenaway's film has thus been almost as diverse and eclectic as its own choice of cultural references.

---

[71] Denham, *The Films of Peter Greenaway*, p. 8.

[72] M. E. Warlick, 'Art, Allegory and Alchemy in Peter Greenaway's *Prospero's Books*', in *New Directions in Emblem Studies*, edited by Amy Wygant (Glasgow: Glasgow Emblem Studies, 1999) pp. 109–136, p. 110.

[73] Coursen, *Watching Shakespeare on Television*, p. 171.

[74] Voigts-Virchow, 'Something richer, stranger, more self-indulgent', pp. 83 and 84.

forbidden planet

....

Forbidden Planet too has generated a vigorous critical response. Seth Lerer begins his analysis of the film by declaring that 'Perhaps the most esteemed science fiction movie of the 1950s, Forbidden Planet has long been appreciated for its blend of high culture allusion and high camp effects'.[75] J. P. Telotte declares that 'Forbidden Planet adds a new dimension, a reflexive element that suggests its direct lineage to recent works like The Running Man (1987) and Robocop (1987), with their explicit subtexts about the media and its role in shaping our culture, and their implicit commentary on film itself'; he argues that 'we might see in Forbidden Planet a paradigm for many of our more recent science fiction films', amongst which he includes Blade Runner.[76] In so far as there are marked parallels between Caliban and Tolkien's Gollum, the second and third films of Peter Jackson's Lord of the Rings can also be seen as in the same tradition. (This is a comparison made by

[75] Seth Lerer, 'Forbidden Planet and the Terrors of Philology', Raritan 19.3 (Winter 2000), pp. 73–86, p. 73.

[76] J. P. Telotte, 'Science Fiction in Double Focus: Forbidden Planet', Film Criticism 13.3 (1989), pp. 25–36, pp. 27–28.

Tolkien himself, when he wrote to his son Christopher that Sam 'treats Gollum rather like Ariel to Caliban',[77] and which others have since drawn: 'The shadow is on the other side of our psyche, the dark brother of the conscious mind. It is Cain, Caliban, Franken-stein's monster, Mr Hyde. It is Vergil who guided Dante through hell, Gilgamesh's friend Enkidu, Frodo's enemy Gollum'.)[78] Unsurprisingly, then, John Jolly says 'Not until the release of MGM's *2001: A Space Odyssey* in 1968 would a science fiction film exploit mythic themes with such consummate artistry as *Forbidden Planet*'.[79]

Forbidden Planet has produced some very interesting critical analyses (including Lerer's own, discussed more fully in Section Two of this book). Anthony Miller argues,

In writing *The Tempest* it seems likely that Shakespeare sought to exploit the advanced theatrical machinery and facilities that may have been on offer at the Blackfriars theatre, recently leased by his company. If so, his project is answered by the striking special effects created for *Forbidden Planet*.

In particular, Miller suggests that

The Tempest of 1610 was written under the impact of the new age of European empire. *Forbidden Planet* of 1956 was written under the impact of the new age of nuclear energy, and in particular nuclear warfare.[80]

[77] Humphrey Carpenter, ed. *The Letters of J. R. R. Tolkien* (London: George Allen & Unwin, 1981), p. 77.

[78] Ursula K. Le Guin, *The Language of the Night* (New York: Putnam, 1979), p. 9.

[79] John Jolly, 'The Bellerophon Myth and *Forbidden Planet*', *Extrapolation* 27.1 (1986), pp. 84–90, p. 89.

[80] Miller, '"In this last tempest"', pp. 26 and 29.

Robert E. Morsberger argues similarly:

The Tempest was science-fiction or at least fantasy-fiction for its seventeenth-century audience, to whom the far Bermoothes were the outer realms of space. And as some modern critics complain of motion picture monsters and marvels, so classicist Ben Jonson complained of Shakespeare's presentation of wonders and objected that with Caliban, Shakespeare graced the stage with monsters.[81]

J. P. Telotte points out that there is considerable evidence of craft in the film, particularly in its representation of doubles:

There is ... a doubled perspective ... as well as doubled characters, repeated actions, and most importantly a thematic concern with duplication or imitation that comes to focus in a series of doubles for the central figure, the stranded scientist Dr Morbius ... These creations not only link this film to a long tradition of doubles and artificial beings in the science fiction genre. They also provide the terms through which *Forbidden Planet* can comment on the usual perspective of the science fiction film and eventually reveal a lack in the double, a danger in the simulacrum that justifies the warning its title sounds.

Declaring that 'Morbius not only fashioned a more effective replacement for his human companions ... he also built in a seemingly unlimited capacity for duplication', Telotte suggests that 'the double replaces the original, the "new" becomes the "original"'.

[81] Robert E. Morsberger, 'Shakespeare and Science Fiction', *Shakespeare Quarterly* 12.2 (1961), p. 161.

Finally, he points to the extradiegetic resonances of this: 'as the lights go out on the rows of power panels surrounding him, as the film's special effects dissipate, so too does Morbius' double disappear', and 'the C57D must speed its passengers away, millions of miles out in space, from where they safely view this destruction. It is, of course, what we too do at this point'.[82]

In 'The Triple Paternity of *Forbidden Planet*', Merrell Knighten offers a sensitive discussion of how 'Morbius, if no longer quite Prospero, is a more tragic protagonist, a Prospero perhaps without the original's firm control of his Caliban, his id, his own primal urges'; 'Without restraint, Shakespeare insists, Caliban is what we might, perhaps would, all become. Without the discipline of the superego, Freudian psychology tells us, the ravening, raging id-beast is what we all are'. Knighten echoes the methodology of New Historicism, which sees the licensed production of subversion as an essential tactic in an overall strategy of containment, when he argues that 'It is this celebration of order that makes Caliban so necessary to *The Tempest*, that makes his Freudian reincarnation so imperative to *Forbidden Planet*', and he uses its language again when he declares that 'Prospero is successful because he has power ... Such success, though, is antithetical to one of the most time-and-practice-hallowed traditions of the science fiction film'. For Knighten, then,

> *Forbidden Planet* is therefore no *Tempest* in its theme, despite its clothing of situation and character, no celebration of power and self-discipline but rather a cautionary moral fable: the transgressor – and Morbius clearly does transgress, both in his barely suppressed incestuous longings and through his initiation into forbidden knowledge – must and will suffer for it.

[82] Telotte, 'Science Fiction in Double Focus: *Forbidden Planet*', pp. 26, 29 and 32.

Indeed Knighten sees *Doctor Faustus* as an influence almost as important as *The Tempest*. 'The result is Shakespearean in its inspiration and framework, Freudian in its method, and Marlovian in its destination – the legitimate single issue of three fathers'.[83] Robert F. Willson also sees *Doctor Faustus* as an influence: he argues that '*Forbidden Planet* recontextualizes the Faustian myth that is the foundation for Shakespeare's romance' and that 'If Morbius is no Prospero, the end of the film perhaps emphasizes how much both of them are like Faustus'.[84] (As John Trushell points out, it is perhaps suggestive that in *Return to Forbidden Planet*, Ferdinand quotes *Doctor Faustus* when Miranda kisses him.)[85]

[83] Merrell Knighten, 'The Triple Paternity of *Forbidden Planet*', *Shakespeare Bulletin* 12.3 (summer, 1994), pp. 36–37, pp. 36 and 37.

[84] Willson, *Shakespeare in Hollywood, 1929–1956*, pp. 102 and 108.

[85] John Trushell, 'A Postmodern (Re)Turn to *Forbidden Planet*', *Foundation* 69 (1997), pp. 60–67, p. 62

afterlife

••

To some extent, Mike Figgis's *Hotel* (2001) can be seen as part of the afterlife of Jarman's *The Tempest*, since it once again offers a Renaissance text (a group of actors are making a film of Webster's *The Duchess of Malfi*), Heathcote Williams (who wrote the script as well as appearing in the film) and much use of blue filters. However, *Forbidden Planet* is alone among the adaptations discussed in this book in having a significant afterlife. Robby the Robot, who, as J. P. Telotte remarks, 'marks a significant turning point for the robot in film, which had previously been largely relegated to sinister roles',[86] appeared in the film *The Invisible Boy* (1957) and had a cameo in *Gremlins* (in the background at an inventors' convention). *Babylon 5* and *Lost in Space* both owe something to *Forbidden Planet* (the robot B in Lost in Space was, like Robby the Robot, designed by Robert Kinoshita); the musical *Return to the Forbidden Planet*, which was billed as 'Shakespeare's Forgotten Rock and Roll Masterpiece' and in which 'Members of the cast converse in broken Shakespearese with dashes of incongrous *sci-fi-isms* from B movies of the 1950s',[87] obviously owes even more. In Douglas

[86] Telotte, 'Science Fiction in Double Focus: *Forbidden Planet*', p. 28.
[87] Trushell, 'A Postmodern (Re)Turn to *Forbidden Planet*'.

Adams's *The Hitchhiker's Guide to the Galaxy*, Ford Prefect prides himself on the fact that he 'knew how to see the Marvels of the Universe for less than thirty Altarian dollars a day'; although Altair is a star in its own right, so that this is not necessarily a reference to *Forbidden Planet*, there is a striking similarity between the crew of the *Bellerophon* landing on Altair IV and Ford and his companions arriving at Magrathea.[88]

Another notable spinoff of *Forbidden Planet* is episode 76 of the original series of *Star Trek*, *Requiem for Methuselah*, first aired in 1969. Although Ruth Morse argues that 'One might look at the situation, in the broad psychological sense, of *King Lear* as much as that of *The Tempest* via *Forbidden Planet*',[89] Allan Asherman observes:

> The story outline for this episode contained some touches that are reminiscent of the classic science fiction film *Forbidden Planet* ... Flint's home was of futuristic design, guarded by Flint's all-purpose robot. In one scene, Kirk and McCoy attempted to sneak into Flint's home to look around: when Flint's robot discovered them, Reena stopped it from attacking them. As Kirk embraced Reena, Dr McCoy guarded the doorway. Finally, Kirk fought a monster that was actually an illusion thrown around Flint's robot.[90]

At the beginning of the episode, a robot (whom we later discover to be named M4) heaves into view just as Kirk, Spock and McCoy

[88] Douglas Adams, *The Hitchhiker's Guide to the Galaxy* (London: Pan, 1979), pp. 15 and 129.

[89] Ruth Morse, 'Monsters, Magicians, Movies: *The Tempest* and the Final Frontier', *Shakespeare Survey* 53 (2000), pp. 164–174, p. 171.

[90] Allan Asherman, *The Star Trek Compendium* (London: W H Allen & Co, 1983), p. 169. Asherman spells the name of the heroine Reena; however, the credits at the end of the episode clearly say 'Rayna'.

have landed. While the robot gathers the mineral they require (and later processes it), the three of them accompany Flint to his home, where they find, amongst other things, a Shakespeare First Folio. Flint (James Daly) proves to have a companion, Rayna (Louise Sorel), who declares 'At last I have seen other humans' and reveals that she has been taught by Flint, thus seeming to fit exactly into the Miranda role. Unlike Alta, she is an intellectual, but just like her, she is drawn to the captain. Flint invites them first to play chess and then to dance together; he watches this, and continues to do so, via a form of closed-circuit TV, when Kirk teaches Rayna to kiss. This voyeuristic behaviour is accounted for when Flint speaks to himself of the captain's 'usefulness', apparently in awakening Rayna.

Other similarities to *Forbidden Planet* include the fact that Flint has a laboratory, and that psychic energy seems to work on this planet (since when the M4 robot interrupts Kirk and Rayna kissing, Rayna muses that 'My mind could not have summoned it'). However, there are also differences. The *Star Trek* episode reintroduces the idea of books, which *Forbidden Planet* itself entirely omits; there are two M4s; and when the three men enter Flint's lab they discover the 'bodies' of 16 previous experiments in making a Rayna-android, lying as if in a morgue. When Flint finds Kirk and McCoy in his laboratory, looking at the 'bodies', he miniaturises the Enterprise: thus the two holy grails of modern technology, miniaturisation and replication, are both neatly delivered. Ironically, it is the non-human Spock who realises that Flint loves the android Rayna, but when Rayna, faced with an agonising choice, implodes as Robbie nearly did when caught between a direct order and his earlier programming, she reveals that falling in love has effectively made her human. For the scriptwriters of *Star Trek* as much as for the audiences at the Globe and Blackfriars, then, *The Tempest* still invites us to ask questions about what it means to be human.

works cited

∙∙

Adams, Douglas, *The Hitchhiker's Guide to the Galaxy* (London: Pan, 1979).

Anderegg, Michael, *Cinematic Shakespeare* (Lanham, MD: Rowman & Littlefield, 2004).

Andreas, James, ' "Where's the Master?": The Technologies of the Stage, Book, and Screen in *The Tempest* and *Prospero's Books*', in *Shakespeare Without Class: Misappropriations of Cultural Capital*, ed. Donald K Hedrick and Bryan Reynolds (Basingstoke: Palgrave, 2000), pp. 189–208.

Asherman, Allan, *The Star Trek Compendium* (London: W H Allen & Co, 1983).

Babula, William, 'Claribel, Tunis and Greenaway's *Prospero's Books*', *Journal of the Wooden O Symposium* (2001), pp. 19–25.

Baden-Powell, Robert, *Scouting for Boys*, ed. Elleke Boehmer (Oxford: Oxford University Press, 2004).

Baker, David J., 'Where is Ireland in *The Tempest*?', in *Shakespeare and Ireland: History, Politics, Culture*, ed. Mark Thornton Burnett and Ramona Wray (Basingstoke: Macmillan, 1997), pp. 68–88.

Barker, Adam, 'A Tale of Two Magicians', in *Film/Literature/ Heritage: A Sight and Sound Reader*, ed. Ginette Vincendeau (London: British Film Institute, 2001), pp. 109–115.

Barker, Francis, and Peter Hulme, 'Nymphs and reapers heavily vanish: the discursive con-texts of *The Tempest*', in *Alternative Shakespeares*, ed. John Drakakis (London: Methuen, 1985), pp. 191–205.

Bennett, Susan, *Performing Nostalgia: Shifting Shakespeare and the Contemporary Past* (London: Routledge, 1996).

Biskind, Peter, *Seeing is Believing: How Hollywood Taught us to Stop Worrying and Love the Fifties* (London: Pluto Press, 1983).

Blumberg, Jane, *Mary Shelley's Early Novels* (Basingstoke: Macmillan, 1993).

Boose, Lynda E., '*The Taming of the Shrew*, Good Husbandry, and Enclosure', in *Shakespeare Reread: The Texts in New Contexts*, ed. Russ McDonald (Ithaca: Cornell University Press, 1994), pp. 193–225.

Brockbank, Philip, '*The Tempest*: Conventions of Art and Empire', in *Later Shakespeare* – Stratford-upon-Avon Studies 8 (London: Edward Arnold, 1966), pp. 183–202.

Brockelman, Thomas P., *The Frame and the Mirror: On Collage and the Postmodern* (Evanston: Northwestern University Press, 2001).

Brotton, Jerry, '"This Tunis, sir, was Carthage": Contesting colonialism in *The Tempest*', in *Post-Colonial Shakespeares*, ed. Ania Loomba and Martin Orkin (London: Routledge, 1998). pp. 23–42.

Brown, Paul, '"This thing of darkness I acknowledge mine": *The Tempest* and the discourse of colonialism', in *Political Shakespeare*, ed. Jonathan Dollimore and Alan Sinfield (Manchester: Manchester University Press, 1985), pp. 48–71.

Bruster, Douglas, 'The Postmodern Theater of Paul Mazursky's *Tempest*', in *Shakespeare, Film, Fin-de-Siècle*, ed. Mark Thornton

Burnett and Ramona Wray (Basingstoke: Macmillan, 2000), pp. 26–39.

Buchanan, Judith, 'Cantankerous Scholars and the Production of a Canonical Text: The Appropriation of Hieronymite Space in *Prospero's Books*', in *Peter Greenaway's Prospero's Books: Critical Essays*, ed. Christel Stalpaert (Ghent: Academia Press, 2000), pp. 43–85.

——. '*Forbidden Planet* and the Retrospective Attribution of Intentions', in *Retrovisions: Reinventing the Past in Film and Fiction*, ed. Deborah Cartmell, I. Q. Hunter, and Imelda Whelehan (London: Pluto, 2001), pp. 148–162.

——. *Shakespeare on Film* (Longman: Pearson, 2005).

Butler, Martin, 'Prospero in Cyberspace', in *Re-constructing the Book: Literary texts in transmission*, ed. Maureen Bell, Shirley Chew, Simon Eliot, Lynette Hunter and James L. W. West III (Aldershot: Ashgate, 2002), pp. 184–196.

Caroti, Simone, 'Science Fiction, *Forbidden Planet*, and Shakespeare's *The Tempest*', in *Comparative Literature and Culture* 6.1 (March, 2004).
Online: http://clcwebjournal.lib.purdue.edu/clcweb04-1/caroti04.html

Carpenter, Humphrey, ed. T*he Letters of J. R. R. Tolkien* (London: George Allen & Unwin, 1981).

Cartelli, Thomas, 'Prospero in Africa: *The Tempest* as colonialist text and precept', in *Shakespeare Reproduced*, ed. Jean E Howard and Marion F. O'Connor (London: Methuen, 1987), pp. 99–115.

——. *Repositioning Shakespeare: National formations, postcolonial appropriations* (London: Routledge, 1999).

Cartmell, Deborah, *Interpreting Shakespeare on Screen*. (Basingstoke: Macmillan, 2000).

Cavecchi, Mariacristina, 'Peter Greenaway's *Prospero's Books*: A Tempest Between Word and Image', in *Literature Film Quarterly* 25.2 (1979), pp. 83–9.

Chedgzoy, Kate, *Shakespeare's Queer Children: Sexual Politics and Contemporary Culture* (Manchester: Manchester University Press, 1995).

Clifton, Michael, 'Cinematic Aliens: Moving Toward the Child', in *Genre at the Crossroads: The Challenge of Fantasy*, ed. George Slusser and Jean-Pierre Barricelli (Riverside, CA: Xenos Books, 2003), pp. 158–166.

Coursen, H. R., *Watching Shakespeare on Television* (London and Toronto: Associated University Presses, 1993).

Curtis, L. Perry Jr, *Apes and Angels: The Irishman in Victorian Caricature* (Newton Abbot: David & Charles, 1971).

Cutts, John P., 'Music and the Supernatural in *The Tempest*', in *Shakespeare, The Tempest: A Casebook*, ed. D. J. Palmer (Basingstoke: Macmillan, 1968), pp. 196–211.

Daileader, Celia R., *Eroticism on the Renaissance Stage: Transcendence, Desire, and the Limits of the Visible* (Cambridge: Cambridge University Press, 1998).

Demaray, John G., *Shakespeare and the Spectacles of Strangeness* (Pittsburgh: Duquesne University Press, 1998).

Denham, Laura, *The Films of Peter Greenaway* (London: Minerva Press, 1993).

DeWeese, Dan, 'Prospero's Pharmacy: Peter Greenaway and the Critics Play Shakespeare's Mimetic Game', in *Almost Shakespeare: Reinventing his Works for Cinema and Television*, ed. James R. Keller and Leslie Stratyner (Jefferson, NC: McFarland and Company, 2004), pp. 155–168.

Dick, Philip K., *Galactic Pot-healer* (London: Gollancz, 2005).

Dillon, Steven, *Derek Jarman and Lyric Film* (Texas: University of Texas Press, 2004).

Donaldson, Peter, 'Digital Archives and Sibylline Fragments: *The Tempest* and the End of Books', in *Postmodern Culture* 8.2 (January 1998). Online (subscription only): http://muse.jhu.edu/journals/postmodern_culture/toc/pmc8.2.html

——. 'Shakespeare in the Age of Post-Mechanical Reproduction: Sexual and electronic magic in *Prospero's Books*', in *Shakespeare, the Movie: Popularizing the plays on film, TV, and video*, ed. Lynda E. Boose and Richard Burt (London: Routledge, 1997), pp. 169–185.

Elliott, J. H., *The Old World and the New 1492–1650* (1970) (Cambridge: Canto, 1992).

Ellis, Jim, 'Conjuring *The Tempest*: Derek Jarman and the Spectacle of Redemption', in *GLQ* 7.2 (2001), pp. 265–84.

Englander, David, Diana Norman, Rosemary O'Day and W. R. Owens, eds., *Culture and Belief in Europe 1450–1600: An Anthology of Sources* (Oxford: Oxford University Press, 1990).

Evans, Malcolm, *Signifying Nothing: Truth's True Contents in Shakespeare's Texts*, 2nd edition (Hemel Hempstead: Harvester, 1989).

Gardner, David, 'Perverse law: Jarman as gay criminal hero', in *By Angels Driven: The Films of Derek Jarman*, ed. Chris Lippard (Trowbridge: Flicks Books, 1996), pp. 31–64.

Gordon, D. J., 'Poet and Architect: The Intellectual Setting of the Quarrel between Ben Jonson and Inigo Jones', in *The Renaissance Imagination: Essays and Lectures by D. J. Gordon*, ed. Stephen Orgel (Berkeley: University of California Press, 1975), pp. 77–101.

Greenaway, Peter, *Prospero's Books: A Film of Shakespeare's* The Tempest (London: Chatto & Windus, 1991).

——. *Prospero's Subjects* (Kamakura: Yobisha Co Ltd, 1992).

Greenblatt, Stephen, 'Invisible bullets: Renaissance authority and its subversion: *Henry IV* and *Henry V*', in *Political Shakespeare*, ed. Jonathan Dollimore and Alan Sinfield (Manchester: Manchester University Press, 1985), pp. 18–47.

——. *Marvelous Possessions* (Oxford: The Clarendon Press, 1991).

Hadfield, Andrew, and Willy Maley, 'Introduction: Irish representations and English alternatives', in *Representing Ireland: Literature and the Origins of Conflict, 1534–1660*, ed. Brendan Bradshaw, Andrew Hadfield, and Willy Maley (Cambridge: Cambridge University Press, 1993), pp. 1–23.

Hart, Jonathan, *Columbus, Shakespeare, and the Interpretation of the New World* (New York: Palgrave, 2003).

Haspel, Paul, 'Ariel and Prospero's Modern-English Adventure: Language, Social Criticism, and Adaptation in Paul Mazursky's *Tempest*', in *Literature/Film Quarterly* 34.2 (2006), pp. 130–139.

Hattaway, Michael, 'Drama and society', in *The Cambridge Companion to English Renaissance Drama*, ed. A. R. Braunmuller and Michael Hattaway (Cambridge: Cambridge University Press, 1990).

Hawkes, David, '"The shadow of this time": the Renaissance cinema of Derek Jarman', in *By Angels Driven: The Films of Derek Jarman*, ed. Chris Lippard (Trowbridge: Flicks Books, 1996), pp. 103–116.

Healy, Thomas, *New Latitudes: Theory and English Renaissance Literature* (London: Edward Arnold, 1992).

Hotchkiss, Lia M., 'The Incorporation of Word as Image in Peter Greenaway's *Prospero's Books*', in *The Reel Shakespeare: Alternative Cinema and Theory*, ed. Lisa S. Starks and Courtney

Lehmann (Cranbury, NJ: Associated University Presses, 2002), pp. 95–117.

Howard, Tony, 'Shakespeare's Cinematic Offshoots', in *The Cambridge Companion to Shakespeare on Film*, ed. Russell Jackson (Cambridge: Cambridge University Press, 2000), pp. 295–313.

Hulme, Peter, *Colonial Encounters: Europe and the Native Caribbean 1492–1797* (London: Methuen, 1986).

Jackson, Russell, 'Shakespeare's Comedies on Film', in *Shakespeare and the Moving Image: The Plays on Film and Television*, ed. Anthony Davies and Stanley Wells (Cambridge: Cambridge University Press, 1994), pp. 99–120.

Jarman, Derek, *Dancing Ledge*, ed. Shaun Allen (London: Quartet Books, 1984).

Jolly, John, 'The Bellerophon Myth and *Forbidden Planet*', *Extrapolation* 27.1 (1986), pp. 84–90.

Klein, Herbert, '"The far side of the mirror": Peter Greenaway's *Prospero's Books*', *Erfurt Electronic Studies in English* (1996). Online: http://webdoc.sub.gwdg.de/edoc/ia/eese/eese.html

Knighten, Merrell, 'The Triple Paternity of *Forbidden Planet*', in *Shakespeare Bulletin* 12.3 (summer, 1994), pp. 36–37.

Lanier, Douglas, 'Drowning the Book: *Prospero's Books* and the Textual Shakespeare', in *Shakespeare on Film: Contemporary Critical Essays*, ed. Robert Shaughnessy (Basingstoke: Palgrave, 1998), pp. 173–195.

Lawrence, Amy, *The Films of Peter Greenaway* (Cambridge: Cambridge University Press, 1997).

Lawson, Chris, 'The Greenawayan Sensory Experience: The Interdependency of Image, Music, Text and Voice as Interconnected

Networks of Knowledge and Experience', in *Peter Greenaway's Prospero's Books: Critical Essays*, ed. Christel Stalpaert (Ghent: Academia Press, 2000), pp. 141–159.

Le Guin, Ursula K., *The Language of the Night* (New York: Putnam, 1979).

Lerer, Seth, '*Forbidden Planet* and the Terrors of Philology', *Raritan* 19.3 (Winter 2000), pp. 73–86.

Loomba, Ania, *Gender, Race, Renaissance Drama* (Manchester: Manchester University Press, 1989).

McCombe, John P., '"Suiting the Action to the Word": The Clarendon *Tempest* and the Evolution of a Narrative Silent Shakespeare', in *Literature/Film Quarterly* 33.2 (2005), pp. 142–155.

MacCabe, Colin, 'A Post-National European Cinema: A Consideration of Derek Jarman's *The Tempest* and *Edward II*', in *Shakespeare on Film: Contemporary Critical Essays*, ed. Robert Shaughnessy (Basingstoke: Palgrave, 1998), pp. 145–155.

Marshall, Tristan, *Theatre and empire: Great Britain on the London stages under James VI and I* (Manchester: Manchester University Press, 2000).

Marston, John, *Antonio and Mellida*, in *The Malcontent and Other Plays*, ed. Keith Sturgess (Oxford: Oxford University Press, 1997).

Martin, Sara, 'Classic Shakespeare for All: *Forbidden Planet* and *Prospero's Books*, Two Screen Adaptations of *The Tempest*', in *Classics in Film and Fiction*, ed. Deborah Cartmell, I. Q. Hunter, Heidi Kaye and Imelda Whelehan (London: Pluto, 2000), pp. 34–53.

Marx, Steven, 'Progeny: *Prospero's Books*, Genesis and *The Tempest*', *Renaissance Forum* 1.2 (September 1996). Online: http://www.hull.ac.uk/renforum/v1no2/marx.htm

——. 'Greenaway's Books', *Early Modern Literary Studies* 7.2 (September, 2001).

Online: http://www.shu.ac.uk/emls/07-2/marxgree.htm

Miller, Anthony, '"In this last tempest": Modernising Shakespeare's *Tempest* on Film', *Sydney Studies in English* 23 (1997), pp. 24–40.

Montrose, Louis, 'The Work of Gender in the Discourse of Discovery', *Representations* 33 (winter, 1991), pp. 1–41.

Morsberger, Robert E., 'Shakespeare and Science Fiction', in *Shakespeare Quarterly* 12.2 (1961), pp. 161.

Morse, Ruth, 'Monsters, Magicians, Movies: *The Tempest* and the Final Frontier, *Shakespeare Survey* 53 (2000), pp. 164–174.

Newman, Karen, '"And wash the Ethiop white": femininity and the monstrous in *Othello*', in *Shakespeare Reproduced*, ed. Jean E. Howard and Marion F. O'Connor (London: Methuen, 1987), pp. 143–62.

Nicholl, Charles, *The Creature in the Map* (1995) (London: Vintage, 1996).

Orr, John, 'The Art of National Identity: Peter Greenaway and Derek Jarman', in *British Cinema, Past and Present*, ed. Justine Ashby and Andrew Higson (London: Routledge, 2000), pp. 327–338.

Pencak, William, *The Films of Derek Jarman* (Jefferson, NC: McFarland & Co, 2002).

Phelan, Peggy, 'Numbering Prospero's Books', *Performing Arts Journal* 14.2 (1992), pp. 43–50.

Pilkington, Ace, 'Zeffirelli's Shakespeare', in *Shakespeare and the Moving Image: The Plays on Film and Television*, ed. Anthony Davies and Stanley Wells (Cambridge: Cambridge University Press, 1994), pp. 163–179.

Romney, Jonathan, *Review of Prospero's Books*, in *Film/Literature/ Heritage: A Sight and Sound Reader*, ed. Ginette Vincendeau (London: British Film Institute, 2001), pp. 142–5.

Rothwell, Kenneth S., *A History of Shakespeare on Screen*, 2nd ed (Cambridge: Cambridge University Press, 2004).

Schatz-Jacobsen, Claus, '"Knowing I Lov'd My Books": Shakespeare, Greenaway, and the Prosperous Dialectics of Word and Image', in *Screen Shakespeare*, ed. Michael Skovmand (Aarhus: Aarhus University Press, 1994), pp. 132–147.

Schwenger, Peter, 'Prospero's Books and the Visionary Page', *Textual Practice* 8.2 (summer 1994), pp. 268–78.

Shakespeare, William, *The Tempest*, ed. Virginia Mason Vaughan and Alden T. Vaughan (London: Thomas Nelson, 2003).

——. *The Tempest*, ed. Stephen Orgel (Oxford: Oxford University Press, 1994).

Shepherd, Simon, *Marlowe and the Politics of Elizabethan Theatre* (London: Harvester, 1986).

Showalter, Elaine, *Sexual Anarchy: Gender and Culture at the Fin de Siècle* (1990) (London: Bloomsbury, 1991).

Stalpaert, Christel, 'The Artistic Creative Process, its Mythologising Effect and its Apparent Naturalness Called into Question: An Interview with Peter Greenaway', in *Peter Greenaway's Prospero's Books: Critical Essays*, ed. Christel Stalpaert (Ghent: Academia Press, 2000), pp. 27–41.

Steinmetz, Leon, and Peter Greenaway, *The World of Peter Greenaway* (Boston: Journey Editions, 1995).

Stoker, Bram, *The Lady of the Shroud* (1909) (London: Alan Sutton, 1994).

Strachey, William, 'A True Reportory...', in *A Voyage to Virginia in 1609: Two Narratives: Strachey's "True Reportory", Jourdain's*

Discovery of the Bermudas (Charlottesville: University Press of Virginia, 1964).

——. *The Historie of Travell into Virginia Britania* (1612), ed. Louis B Wright and Virginia Freund (London: The Hakluyt Society, 1953).

Telotte, J. P., 'Science Fiction in Double Focus: *Forbidden Planet*', in *Film Criticism* 13.3 (1989), pp. 25–36.

Thompson, Ann, '"Miranda, where's your sister?": Reading Shakespeare's *The Tempest*', in *Feminist Criticism: Theory and Practice*, ed. Susan Sellers (Hemel Hempstead: Harvester Wheatsheaf, 1991), pp. 45–55.

Todorov, Tzvetan, *The Conquest of America: The Question of the Other*, trans. R. Howard (New York: Doubleday, 1984).

Trushell, John, 'A Postmodern (Re)Turn to *Forbidden Planet*', *Foundation* 69 (1997), pp. 60–67.

Tudeau-Clayton, Margaret, *Jonson, Shakespeare, and Early Modern Virgil* (Cambridge: Cambridge University Press, 1998).

Vaughan, Alden T., and Virginia Mason Vaughan, *Shakespeare's Caliban: A Cultural History* (Cambridge: Cambridge University Press, 1991).

Vaughan, Virginia Mason, 'Preface: The Mental Maps of English Renaissance Drama', in *Playing the Globe: Genre and Geography in English Renaissance Drama*, ed. John Gillies and Virginia Mason Vaughan (London: Associated University Presses, 1998), pp. 7–16.

Voigts-Virchow, Eckart, 'Something richer, stranger, more self-indulgent: Peter Greenaway's Fantastic See-Changes in *Prospero's Books* et al.', in *Anglistik und Englischunterricht* 59 (1996), pp. 83–99.

Wall, Geoffrey, 'Greenaway Filming *The Tempest*', *Shakespeare Yearbook* 4 (1994), pp. 335–9.

Warlick, M. E., 'Art, Allegory and Alchemy in Peter Greenaway's *Prospero's Books*', in *New Directions in Emblem Studies,* ed. Amy Wygant (Glasgow: Glasgow Emblem Studies, 1999), pp. 109–136.

Willoquet-Maricondi, Paula, 'Aimé Césaire's *A Tempest* and Peter Greenaway's *Prospero's Books* as Ecological Rereadings and Rewritings of Shakespeare's *The Tempest*', in *Reading the Earth: New Directions in the Study of Literature and Environment,* ed. Michael P Branch, Rochelle Johnson, Daniel Patterson, and Scott Slovic (Moscow, Idaho: University of Idaho Press, 1998). pp. 209–224.

Willson, Robert F., Jr, *Shakespeare in Hollywood, 1929–1956* (London: Associated University Presses, 2000).

Wilson, Daniel, *Caliban: The Missing Link* (London: Macmillan, 1873).

Woods, Alan, *Being Naked Playing Dead: The Art of Peter Greenaway* (Manchester: Manchester University Press, 1996).

Wymer, Rowland, '*The Tempest* and the Origins of Britain', *Critical Survey* 11.1 (1999), pp. 3–14.

——. *Derek Jarman* (Manchester: Manchester University Press, 2005).

Youngs, Tim, 'Cruising against the Id: The Transformation of Caliban in *Forbidden Planet*', in *Constellation Caliban: Figurations of a Character,* ed. Nadia Lie and Theo D'haen (Amsterdam: Rodopi, 1997), pp. 211–229.

Zabus, Chantal, and Kevin A. Dwyer, '"I'll be wise hereafter": Caliban in Postmodern British Cinema', in *Constellation Caliban: Figurations of a Character,* ed. Nadia Lie and Theo D'haen (Amsterdam: Rodopi, 1997), pp. 271–289.

index

••